Winning
Big
In Sales

Proven steps for ambitious teams to win, grow and retain the best accounts

REBECCA JENKINS

Contents

FOREWORD...1

INTRODUCTION..1

PART ONE: WINNING BIG ACCOUNTS 5

1: TARGETING THE RIGHT BUSINESS 6

Preparation for prospecting 6

Steps in the transformational sales process.................................7

Essential planning 8

2: INSIGHTS AND TRANSFORMATIONAL CONCEPTS.........16

Gaining insights...16

Gathering company insights...18

Gathering sector insights 19

3: PROSPECTING WITH IMPACT 25

The powerful prospecting combination 26

Prospecting telephone call structure 29

Brand and congruency 34

4: SUCCESSFUL PROSPECTING MEETINGS 38

Presenting your ideas...38

Qualifying your target..39

No objections, no questions, no win 40

Prospecting meeting structure 44

5: WINNING THE BIG ACCOUNT 54

Your proposal..54

The transformational close 56

The follow-up 61

Dealing with radio silence...62

Winning and contractual negotiations 64

PART TWO: GROWING AND KEEPING BIG ACCOUNTS 68

6: A TURNING POINT AND MY BIGGEST BUSINESS LESSON EVER 69

About to lose a big account 70

Selecting the best account for transformation 74

7: TRANSFORMATION 82

Assessing your client relationship 82

Considerations to finding a transformational project 86

Presenting your transformational project to gain traction 87

The power of story 90

8: LAUNCHING AND LEADING 97

The TP project kick off with your client's team 97

Relationship essentials 98

9: SUCCESS MINDSET 106

Staying focused 106

Your vision 108

The evidence 108

Managing your mind for success 110

FINAL SUMMARY 114

ACKNOWLEDGEMENTS 116

ABOUT REBECCA 117

RESOURCES 118

FOREWORD

The driver for how my professional relationship began with Rebecca Jenkins, stems from one career changing transformational project.

I have spent most of my career building logistics solutions and services within a singular framework, enhancing the customer proposition for the individual business I was working for. When our project launched, we opened up our logistics and retail networks to other third parties. Suddenly we were a commercial start-up, a service provider, competing against well-established, scaled, multi-million pound businesses who were dominant in their sector.

Rebecca heavily supported my team on its journey, helping us find clarity of purpose and pragmatism to achieve results that are beyond industry expectations.

In this book, Rebecca has distilled over 20 years' business experience of how to acquire, grow and retain *Big Accounts*. The book will help you organise and refine your approach, give you practical steps to succeed and ultimately even the playing field – enabling you and your organisation to punch above its weight.

If you follow the principles outlined here, you will achieve some amazing results – *it is a masterclass.*

Paul Anastasiou
Senior Director Asda Logistics

WINNING BIG IN SALES

INTRODUCTION

My Promise to you, the reader.

Thank you for choosing this book. It is dedicated to all those of you who are involved in the challenging yet immensely enjoyable path of winning new business in the business to business (B2B) environment. Whether that be for a sales, business development or account management role. It is also for other business leaders with a desire to raise the bar and win bigger accounts for their business. I'm going to show you how to do that step by step, because winning, growing and keeping large prestigious accounts doesn't have to be reserved for your competitors. You can compete and win, even if the size of your business is smaller in comparison. Even if the economy is tough or if your rivals are more cost competitive.

Winning big and valuable accounts brings many benefits. The ability to scale a business because you have a contractual commitment on which to project future growth and financial returns. You will increase other opportunities for growth because in doing a great job, your client will ask you first to be considered for other projects. Then there is the recognition of working with well-known bigger companies which brings enhanced credibility, often opening the door to work with other large businesses.

Winning, growing and renewing big contracts brings personal kudos too. You can earn a reputation as a high achiever. Doing what might have been considered impossible by others can help catapult your career and your earning potential.

My very first sales role was over 25 years ago and the excitement of winning a big account has never worn off. I'm as excited by it today as I was in those early days, even if the win is on behalf of the companies I work with. It was the sense of achievement from my first decent sales win when I realised that I would enjoy a career where sales would be a large part of the role. Fortunately, that has been the case, but little did I know about the challenges that lay ahead. That I would work with and learn from exceptional leaders. Such as the late Dame Anita Roddick of The Body Shop and management guru Tom Peters, both of whom have impacted my approach to winning and keeping clients.

I wrote this book because I wanted to share what I've learnt from the highs and lows of winning big exciting accounts with companies such as Next, The Body Shop and Magnet. Beating the largest players in the industry to whom all the big contracts typically went, because they were seen as the safe bet. The appointing executive wouldn't lose their job, because in selecting a top tier company, they'd made a 'sensible' choice. This squashed the opportunities for smaller businesses who may have been equally as good if not better.

I faced such challenges in growing a business to £55 million in sales revenue. For a long time, we didn't win the large accounts I wanted. We were often told by the prospective clients that we were unable to replicate what the big players could offer. Being determined to win one of them, we eventually had our lucky break and secured a big account with a prominent retailer. Unexpectedly, 12 months later we were precariously close to losing it and this would have had serious business implications. It is often said that in your bleakest hour comes your breakthrough. I can vouch for that now, as it led me to my new approach of transforming sales results.

The techniques and methods in this book come from tough lessons learnt and real experience. From understanding the reasons behind our losses as well as our profitable and successful wins. From these experiences we become more successful at acquiring and growing big valuable accounts. It wasn't just in winning them, but also in discovering how to keep them long term, some for over 15 years. In this book I have mapped out the process, so you too can do it.

Each chapter builds on the last, so if you're an account manager who doesn't have to win new business from scratch, I still recommend that you read part one on winning new accounts. This is because the research and analysis is also applied to the process of growing your existing accounts.

I'm often asked, how quickly can results be expected? The quickest time that I have applied this process and won a big account is three months. The client didn't already have a contract in place with another supplier as it was for a brand new development.

Often by their very nature, big accounts have a length of time where they are contractually obligated to stay with the current supplier before the contractual term ends. This can dictate how long it will take to win a big account. The time between a contract finishing and the re-tender process is rich ground for sowing seeds that you later harvest. Putting to one side any contractual timeframes, you will benefit from the techniques in this book, as there are less steps compared to the traditional sales process.

Building a pipeline of big account prospects is important, so that you have opportunities at different stages in the sales funnel. I will take you through the whole process: how to identify the right prospects that will be an asset to your business, how to approach, win and keep them. I will show you how to attain a new level, a new high of selling. One which will have a significant positive impact on your business.

Often people who aren't in sales attach negative labels to people in sales, giving it a poor reputation. This is because anyone who has witnessed an aggressive sales approach can be left unhappy by the experience. Professional salespeople don't operate this way; they are looking for ways to improve and refine their performance and skills. They strive to find clients for the long term, those who are a good fit for their business and who become loyal advocates of the company. This book builds on that professionalism.

I've always considered that the responsibility you undertake in a sales role is not for the faint hearted as it requires bravery and boldness. You have to get out there and make it happen. As sales and business development professionals, you have to not only win new clients but find the right ones. Those clients that operations will be delighted with, an age-old challenge and that your team will thank you for.

It's not about finding business at any cost or bringing in a quick win to improve your sales ratios. The focus has to be on finding accounts that are a great fit because they add value to the business and support its strategic plans. This book shows you how to do that.

Earlier, I mentioned the risk of losing a hard-won prestigious key account after just 12 months of winning it. Having beaten our biggest rivals to secure it, losing it would have had a serious impact on the business. The experience left me feeling as if I had been punched in the body by a heavy weight boxing champion.

You'll find out more about this, how we won it and what we did, in chapter six.

Thankfully, this experience led me to my biggest sales 'ah ha' moment. It changed the way I approached sales from there on in. It enabled me to grow a business and win many big accounts, ones which were usually only awarded to our largest competitors. This was a transformational approach to gaining new business. Achieved despite the uncertain times of two recessions and having fewer resources than those we competed against.

If in your role you have responsibility for growing existing accounts, then this book will give you a proven approach to achieving big account growth, as well as how to keep your accounts for many years to come.

If you are new to sales you will benefit from the concepts and techniques in this book, but I'd also encourage you to become competent in basic sales principles and master those to supplement what you learn here.

If you are a business owner or leader of a smaller company, you can be influential in the sales process. Combining the techniques in this book with your leadership skills, will make the winning of big accounts a rewarding part of business life.

This methodology is solid. It has been repeated, refined and applied across different sectors and it delivers impressive results. With sophisticated buyers in business today, sophisticated sales methods are needed. This doesn't mean complicated. My approach is straightforward, it requires planning & research, but that pays off in the results.

I think you will be pleased that there are less steps in the sales process. Delighted that it replaces the traditional sales discovery meeting with a more effective approach. Over the moon that it doesn't require extra resources! The added benefit is that in implementing these techniques you can enjoy more of those triumphant and delightful moments that come with achieving important and significant sales success.

My next promise to you is that you will not only have a method for winning retaining and keeping big accounts. You will also understand the role that your mind plays, in making your success happen faster and with more ease. We are beginning to understand through research into neuroscience, that the way we *programme* our mind plays a significant role in our success.

I will take you through how you can achieve this and explain the science behind it. This, couple with the methods in this book, has benefitted others, who along with the methods in this book have enjoyed transformational results that they never considered to be possible.

I once heard one of my clients, the VP of sales in a global technology business say that, "The best salespeople don't sell". This statement I empathetically agree with. I know that this might sound ridiculous as we launch into a book about sales and winning big accounts.

It doesn't mean that you don't need to know about selling, or how to apply sales techniques, but it does say everything about my approach. The hard sell is out and achieving exciting sales growth through insights and transformation is in.

4

PART ONE:
WINNING BIG ACCOUNTS

CHAPTER 1: TARGETING THE RIGHT BUSINESS

The sales approach in this book is transformational both for your client and your business. It transforms an aspect of the prospect's or client's business which is directly related to improving what is important to their strategy and business drivers. For your company, it enables you to achieve big wins with clients who are a great fit for the business and in sectors that have growth potential and are most viable. This transformation requires research, thought and new ideas. This is achieved effectively by following the process detailed in the next two chapters.

You might prefer to read the chapter through first, then return to do the exercises. They are important to do because they form the foundation of winning big accounts.

My favourite all-time big account win was with The Body Shop. They, like our other big account wins, didn't call me and ask me to quote for their distribution. We had to go out there and find them, unlike the experience of our largest competitors.

They, because of their scale and standing as a tier-one provider, had the luxury of tenders coming directly to them frequently. If you're a smaller business, you have to play a different game to get such opportunities. The good news is that you can win big accounts It takes some essential preparation, which we go through in this chapter.

Preparation for prospecting

Prospecting is a skill that all salespeople need to master to increase their opportunity of winning new business. Before approaching a company, there is a five-step prospecting preparation process to undertake. This preparation is worth every second invested in it. It pays dividends, as you will be more targeted and able to demonstrate relevant expertise to the prospects you pursue. This enables you to make faster progress.

If you have responsibility for growing existing accounts, elements of this preparation are relevant to achieving transformational growth and account retention. Therefore, it's worth understanding the process.

Steps in the transformational sales process

What makes the transformational sales process better than traditional sales processes is that you immediately add value to the prospect. This increases their interest and engagement, giving you traction in the sales cycle early on. The other advantage is that it has fewer steps in the sales process, making it a more effective approach.

A traditional sales process will follow these steps

1. Attain database of target companies

2. Research before contacting

3. Contact company and qualify need

4. Have discovery meeting and present company to prospect

5. Consider information from discovery meeting to prepare a solution

6. Present solution and proposal

7. Win

> **The steps in the transformational sales process are:**
>
> 1. Pre-prospecting research and analysis for best fit targets
>
> 2. Contact targets for value exchange meetings
>
> 3. Present and validate insights and transformational concept (Here on referred to as TC) tailored to targets strategic goals/business drivers
>
> 4. Present solution and proposal
>
> 5. Win

Each of the sales steps to win big are fully detailed and in chapter one, we start with the first four steps of the pre-prospecting preparation.

Essential planning

This preparation enables you to know which sectors you should target and prioritise. How to research the target companies to increase fit factor and how to be highly relevant in the prospecting process. Time invested here pays off, so don't be tempted to cut corners. Winning big accounts requires preparation.

The process is detailed and will take time to do thoroughly. Once completed, the clarity and focus it provides will dramatically improve your prospecting results.

An overview of the pre-prospecting preparation steps:

1. **Analysis** - analyse the sectors of your current customer base to determine priority sectors to target.
2. **Attractiveness** - complete a market attractiveness analysis.
3. **Capability to convert** - complete a capability to convert to sales analysis.
4. **Target** - use the results from the above steps to create a list of target companies.
5. **Insights** - research targets to gain sector and company insights.
6. **Transformational Concept**- develop a TC using the insights information to present a new way forward.

In this chapter, we are going through steps 1 – 4.

1. Analyse the sectors of your current customer base

The purpose of analysing the sectors of your current customers is twofold. Firstly, to establish which sectors generate the highest level of profitability for your business. Secondly, to evaluate the correlation between profitability and the size of the company. This will give you clarity on the priority sectors to target as you are able to generate good returns there. You will also know the size of companies that generate the best margins, giving you the focus for both sectors and company size to target.

Note: should your analysis show that your larger turnover clients produce less profit margin consider what other benefits they may bring to the business.

This could be:

- More regular business that counteracts seasonal troughs/peaks, which may increase the efficiency of operations.
- They might give you better purchasing power, which will help you win other new clients.
- They can increase your credibility in the market sector, opening up new opportunities to grow your market share.
- They could bring increased brand awareness because they provide opportunities for good press coverage.

All of these benefits are difficult to put a definitive financial figure on, but do consider them when determining the size of company you are going to target.

From this process, you will know which sectors are best to focus on and actively pursue as part of your prospecting.

Quick example

Richard is the sales director at a printing business who provide services across a range of sectors including professional services, education, health and advertising agencies.

He analyses the profit margins on each account and quickly spots that margins are better in health and professional services.

He then looks at the size of companies in each of these sectors and discovers that the margin is better in the smaller companies.

He's initially surprised, then realises that the last-minute demand for printing is a trait of the smaller businesses and this enables him to increase margins. The larger companies provide regular volume to the business and while the margins are lower, it avoids the cost of machinery standing idle. Richard will target both large and small companies in the health and professional services sectors.

Here is the pre-prospecting process to determine the sectors you are going to focus on.

Client sector analysis process:

- List your most profitable clients – take your top 20, or more depending on the number of clients you have.
- Research and note the client's turnover – not their revenue spend with you, but their actual business revenue.
- Detail which sector vertical each client is in, i.e. food manufacturing, fashion retailing, car parts distributor etc.
- Note the profit or gross margin percentage you earn from each client, be consistent with the measure you select.

In the resources section at the back of this book, you can use Template 1 - Sector Analysis Template for this assessment. You can download a copy at rjen.co.uk/downloads

On completion of this analysis, take the top four or five most profitable sectors and move onto step two.

2. Sector attractiveness

You now have a list of your most profitable sectors. You will be investing resources, time, money and energy into prospecting. So, you want the confidence that these sectors are viable for the future and are a good fit for your business.

You can use the sector attractiveness template 2a in the resources section at the back of the book or download a template at www.rjen.co.uk/downloads

As you go through the questions, consider your responses as appropriate and make a note of your answers. You can either jot down your responses to keep track of them or use the market attractiveness/capability to convert template. You will find the template in the resources section at the back of the book. At the end of the questions, you will be adding up how many low, medium and high (or equivalent) answers you have given.

The purpose of this step is to give you that confidence. Next is a series of questions to complete the sector attractiveness analysis.

Success Tip

Remember you are answering the questions about your company in relation to the sector you are focusing on.

Table 1

Answer the sector attractiveness questions to assess how attractive the sector is to your business:

1. **Market share** - What is your share of the market in this sector and is there room for growth and scalability? Answer low, medium or high

An example of a high score would be: we have 25 percent of the European market in this sector. which gives us scope to scale to win new business.

2. **Growth** - To what extent is the market in this sector growing? Is the market mature, in decline or in growth? Answer low, medium or high

An example of a high score would be: the sector is growing at a fast pace and it is expected to mature in 5 years or longer.

3. **Risks** - What are the risks of operating in this sector? These could be political, geographical, labour shortage, regulation, new entrants, economic. Answer low, medium or high.

An example of a high score would be; we have successfully implemented strategies to reduce the risk exposure of working in this sector.

4. **Financial** – Do you have the resources to invest (this could be in technology, machinery, equipment) and achieve acceptable financial returns? Answer (no, potentially or yes)

An example of a yes score would be: we have the resources to invest in this sector and through our sector experience we know we can make good financial returns.

5. **Prices** - Are prices and margins under pressure in this sector? Answer (no, potentially or yes).

An example of a yes answer would be: our product delivers high margins because of our specific area of expertise

When you have completed the questions, use the following scoring to get an overall score/colour for the sector and repeat the process for the other sectors to establish priority sectors to target.

Scoring Key out of 10 - (for both the sector attractiveness and capability to convert questions)	
0-3 = low/no answers	Shade box red
4-6 = medium/possibly/potentially answers	Shade box amber
7- 10 = high/yes answers	Shade box green

The purpose of using colours is that it gives you a strong and clear visual representation.

3. Capability to convert

The same approach now applies to the capability to convert analysis. Consider your responses to the questions and either jot down your answers or use Template 2b - Capability to Convert, in the resources section at the back of this book. You can also download a copy at: www.rjen.co.uk/downloads.

At the end of the questions, measure how many low, medium and high (or equivalent) answers you have given. Use the scoring key above to get an overall score/colour for the sector to establish your capability to convert leads to sales.

Table 2 - Answer the questions below to assess your capability to convert leads to new business.

1. **Competitive advantage** - do you have a strong competitive advantage? For example, this could be differentiation through patented products, cost benefits, location, scale of operation, innovation of product or exceptional client experience. Answer (no, potentially or yes).

An example of a yes answer would be: we have patented methodology or products that reduce wastage in the manufacturing process and we can demonstrate these efficiencies through case studies.

2. **Expertise** – is your knowledge of the sector detailed with relevant expertise and understanding of its challenges? Answer (low, medium or high).

An example of a high score would be: we have years of experience in this sector; we understand its challenges and have sales teams with sector knowledge.

3. **Innovation or added value** – can you evidence innovation or value add with your clients through case studies, testimonials or reports? Answer (no, potentially or yes).

An example of a yes score would be: we have developed, tested and have in operation a new product that shortens the lead time for the manufacture of products. We have won awards for our innovation and it is recognised as a market leader.

4. **Performance** – can you evidence that you deliver performance benefits? These could be cost savings, efficiencies, value for money or expertise, demonstrated through case studies or testimonials. Answer (no, potentially or yes).

An example of a yes score would be: case studies on how our company's specialist knowledge in public relations management and consultancy prevented reputational damage from the leaking of personal data into the public arena.

Table 2 – Continued

5. **Position of brand leadership** – is your company regarded as a leader in the sector? Do you have products designed specifically for the sector? Are you the go-to name for providing solutions in this sector? Answer (no, potentially or yes).

An example of a yes score would be: our software is regarded as one of the go-to software providers for business presentation software and our brand reputation has been consistently high over the last 3 years or more.

Ideal sectors will be where the attractiveness of the market is high or coloured green **and** the capability to convert is green. It's the combined results of both assessments that need to be considered. The sweet spot is where sector attractiveness and capability to convert are high/green. Repeat the process for each of the top 3 – 4 sectors you listed in step 1. This will give you a clear picture of which sectors offer the best opportunity for you to progress and you have the rationale for it too.

4. Targets - research target companies in the most attractive sectors

The next step is to create a target list of 20-50 companies in your priority selected sectors where you have high/green scores. These companies are usually easy to find with a bit of research. Many industry sectors have lists of the largest companies in that market, often a top 100. These may be segmented into various categories, such as most profitable or fastest growing. You can find them in sector-specific journals, via trade associations or their representative professional bodies.

As you create your list, remember to think big. Go for organisations that when you win them as a client, will make a substantial difference to your business. Its reputation, growth and financial performance.

Summary - In this chapter, we've covered:

- The first 4 steps in preparing for prospecting.
- How to evaluate your existing clients to assess which sectors will be the best fit for your business.
- Undertaken a market sector attractiveness and capability to convert analysis to gain a clear priority of the target sectors.
- Researched and created a list of 20-50 sector-specific companies to target.

CHAPTER 2: INSIGHTS AND TRANSFORMATIONAL CONCEPTS

In this chapter, we cover the final steps five and six of the pre-prospecting preparation. It includes how to make your prospecting more impactful so that you get interest, engagement and traction right at the beginning.

This important step is often missed by eager sales teams who just want to get on with the first meeting with a potential client without this important step. In not doing this, they can miss early an opportunity to get the prospects interest, attention and engagement.

5. Pre -prospecting preparation

Gaining insights

Have you had the experience of finding out about something that you didn't know much about, to discover there was a lot more to it than you expected? That's what I call gaining insights and it's the next step in the prospecting preparation process.

There are two sets of insights to be gathered. One being sector and the other being about the target company.

The more you know about the companies on your target list, the more success you will have with prospecting. Let's see how much you can answer about your target prospects already.

Do you know their vision, their plans and goals for this year and the next three? What are they striving to achieve? What new business opportunities are they looking for? Are they planning to create new products or develop new services? Are they looking to break into new sectors?

Do they have growth plans? Have they got a strong executive team and do they have all the skills in house to reach their goals? What do they plan to do more of and less of? What are their weak spots? What is their competitive advantage and what are their economic/business drivers?

Now consider the sectors. You already know if the sector is growing or mature but delve into other aspects. Who are the new entrants to the sector and what are they offering? Is the market being disrupted with new technology or operating methods? What are the trends, pressure points and challenges?

The research into the company and sector insights form a crucial aspect of your prospecting. The more insights you can gather, the more successful your prospecting pitch will be.

If you are responsible for increasing sales on existing accounts, you will benefit from undertaking both the sector and client insights research too. The objective of this step is to get under the skin of your accounts or prospects and their sector. To know specific useful information about both areas. As you are collecting and analysing the data, you need to be thinking about how the data is useful to you. Consider what your company does or could do that will help overcome their challenges. How you can help them achieve their vision and goals, as well as that of their sector, with its trends and opportunities.

This goes beyond solution selling which, by definition, is understanding the prospect's challenges through discovery meetings and then selling solutions. While the principle of this is still important and relevant today, everyone in sales worth their salt is doing this. It's much harder to stand out.

The detailed level of insights research, both prospect and sector analysis, allows you to stand out at the sales meeting, or at the review meeting if you are growing an existing account. Standing out with in-depth insights and knowledge is important and has considerable benefits too. Compared to your competitors, it positions you as credible and therefore better able to create the best solution. Through demonstrating that you understand them and their sector in detail, you will improve your prospecting and each aspect of the sales cycle.

You may think the downside to this approach, is that it's a lot of time invested in research which might not result in business wins. Yes, that is a possibility. However, this approach is more targeted.

By undertaking the research beforehand, you will use the knowledge to show how you add value to prospects even before they become clients. For existing clients, it demonstrates your commitment to providing on-going value and finding new opportunities for growth.

Often the first prospecting meeting is called a discovery meeting to find out about the client.

The transformational approach is more effective. From the beginning, you will have a lot of knowledge already and go into the prospecting meeting with interesting ideas. These ideas lead to useful discussions, which gives you a big lift up the sales engagement ladder.

I call the first prospecting meeting, "Value Exchange Meetings". You're presenting valuable ideas, concepts, innovations and insights that are aligned to the company's bigger goals, purpose and sector. You're receiving valuable feedback that's helping you to progressing an opportunity.

Being forearmed with this knowledge respects the prospect's time. It shows you have some clear and researched ideas about how you can add value. It builds trust more quickly, as you've already demonstrated an investment of time and thought in their business and how you can help them.

The process of gaining insights is easy. As you go through what I've mapped out, you'll build your knowledge quickly and see the advantage it gives you.

Gathering company insights

Background information such as company accounts help to evaluate a company's performance. This will ascertain their financial position and trends in profitability and balance sheet strength. You don't need to be an accountant to take a high-level view of financial performance. This information is available online at Companies House in the United Kingdom.

Read their annual reports and statements. What is their position on culture and values? New developments and Corporate Social Responsibility? What is their business model?
Much of this information can be gleaned from their online presence, their social media posts, press releases and blog posts. You could also talk with employees of the company or sample their product or service.

Understand their key business drivers; these could be gaining market share, improving infrastructure, increasing production capability, reducing machine downtime, developing knowledge and/or improving occupancy rates.

The best research comes from experience!

Your online research is essential. Finding ways to supplement it through experiencing the products or service of the target company adds a new and invaluable dimension to your knowledge.

Here's an example. Let's say your company helps businesses to improve their customer or client experience. You provide consulting services to map out the customer journey and improve it and you have a list of target companies with whom you'd like to do business.

Consider how powerful it would be if you contacted your target companies to see how they handled an enquiry from you. Repeat the process to see if a pattern emerges. Are they consistently good or poor? Is your query handled better in certain regions, or at certain times of the day? Now overlay this with what their customer experience goals are. Is there a gap between those goals and reality? Position your research and reality findings into a report and use that as your insights for an impactful prospecting meeting.

Here are some other examples.

- If you are a packaging company targeting online retailers, purchase the product and examine the condition of the product when it arrives. How would you improve it? Put that information into your prospecting pitch, along with what the potential cost could be of fewer complaints about damaged products. The fact that you can talk from experience about their product will be impressive to your prospect.
- If you manufacture uniforms, examine the uniforms worn by your target company. Do they represent the brand values of the company? Are they clean and crisp or worn and in need of repair? Consider how you could improve the designs, the functionality and longevity of materials. How would it better reflect their brand? Take samples to the prospecting meeting.

Gathering sector insights

With the sector insights, you gain a detailed understanding of the challenges or opportunities of their sector. Combine this with the insights of your target company; you can begin to see the world through their lens. Your aim is to find the golden nugget, the opportunity where you can add value. This could be through product or service innovation, developing an opportunity in response to a new sector trend or market demand, eradicating a problem or reducing costs. Time now to gather these sector insights.

Research the sector and understand its pressure points. These could be legislative, economic, or new disrupters in the sector. Review and consider the trends and projections about its future. You can do this by reading relevant white papers and sector journals. Join sector associations to gain deeper knowledge, attend events and listen to keynote speakers.

At such events, mix with the audience and ask them what challenges their sector is facing. Set up Google Alerts and be notified of developments in the market which will come directly to you in your email. Find experts who know the sector and read their content, books and speeches. Follow them on social media, connect and seek their opinion or commission them for a report.

Commissioning an independent white paper that evaluates trends in the sector is a good way to gain sector insights. You get visibility of current and future challenges the sector faces.

These insights will be useful to you and your target companies. The white paper can consider what the impact will be of challenges or trends in the sector and what companies can do to avoid being left behind.

Contacting a local university and offering a research project to MBA students is an excellent way to get this completed, often free of charge or in exchange for a small fee.

An example of using insights:

Here's a good example of how one company used the insights approach to win an opportunity with a UK retailer. The company, a provider of store fittings and display furniture, commissioned an independent paper on the future of retailing and how a concept store of the future would look.

They took the report to one of their large accounts and presented it to a senior executive. At the end of it, they were asked to provide a proposal to create a concept that would be a flagship store for them.

You can use reports or articles that already exist and build on them, For example I recently read a short report on what retailers need to do to keep loyal customers. The premise of the report was the need to build trust. Nothing new there, but you could use the basis of that report to conduct your own research by asking shoppers if they agree with it.

If you were a branding agency targeting retailers, you have an expert's opinion of the market from the article, which you could develop further. and explain how you could tackle the problem, as well as undertaking some research into which retailers fell into the low trust category.

If I were one of those branding agency's target retailers and you were presenting such useful and interesting insights with a way to tackle the problem at a prospecting meeting, that would be invaluable and certainly grab my attention.

This demonstrates the essence of how you can use insights to develop a transformational concept which we are coming on to in this chapter.

An example of using insights that led to a multi-million pound contract win.

As Managing Director, following the success of securing several prestigious contracts, I set our sights on winning one with a major high street fashion brand.

The process of collecting insights began. We didn't just review their current distribution structure and see if we could improve it, we had to gather wider insights. We needed to understand what frustrated the store managers about the delivery service. as well as what their consumers wanted. Then to consider the relevance and impact of that to the retailers strategic goals and business drivers.

We discovered that the retailer's ability to replenish fast-selling items was slow. If we could restock the stores overnight from their warehouses, the increase in sales would be substantial and far outweigh the costs associated with night-time deliveries.

If we hadn't considered trends in the retail sector and needs of consumers we would have just focused on the here and now. We wouldn't have taken a strategic view that enabled us to develop a transformational concept. A concept that supported the retailer's wider business strategy and future retail landscape.

The result - we won a multi-million pound contract!

In the resources section at the back of this book, you will find Template 3 - Target Company and Sector Insights, to help you with your insights research.

6. Transformational concept

The TC is developed by taking the sector and company insights you have researched. Then use that information to consider how your company could help them to achieve their business goals. You demonstrate to your prospect that your company knows their business and sector, along with its challenges, trends and opportunities. Followed by how you can help them to achieve their goals through your TC.

What you are striving to achieve is an idea for transforming an important aspect of their business that is linked to their key business drivers and/or their strategy– this is the TC.

This concept positions you ahead of your competition. You are now focusing on adding value that will have a transformational impact on your target company, because you understand their sector and business drivers. These are the areas that are important to them and you are going to help to improve them.

Contrast this with going to a prospecting meeting to discover this information. See how it gives you a competitive advantage and changes the whole sales process? You will be leading the conversation; you have valuable and highly relevant information to share. Consider how much more compelling and purposeful your first prospecting meeting will be.

For a moment, put the boot on the other foot. Imagine you had a first meeting with a salesperson and they presented this level of quality insights relevant to your business. Information to improve the aspects of your business that you are important to you. Wouldn't you be willing to give them more time and attention?

Success Tips

Take time to gather insights so that you can create a transformation concept. Just as car manufacturers create concept cars which they test and refine, you will do the same.

Brainstorm transformational ideas with your clients or colleagues who already work in the target sector. This is a good way to get different perspectives helping you to align your insights with a TC. Develop the concept further by discussing it with your prospect at the first meeting.

The importance of getting the right insights and considering them from different angles

I was working with a start up company that had an excellent idea for a new business, which would require them to break into a very traditional market. Surprisingly there were only two major organisations operating in it.

The startup's competitor market research was extensive. It included profiling the financial strength, manufacturing capability, infrastructure and market share of the two dominant companies.

The startup planned to use a low-price offering as their way to get traction and sales in the market. With that strategy, the two dominant players could easily reduce their prices and push the start up out of business. She needed new insights.

She hadn't considered what consumers wanted other than lower prices or how could she get their commitment to her product even if the competitors matched prices? Those were the additional insights needed.

Summary - In this chapter we've covered:

- The final steps in the pre-prospecting process – you are now ready for prospecting with full impact. How to do this is coming up in the next chapter.
- How to gain sector and company insights that are the building blocks to getting attention and engagement in the prospecting meeting.
- How to add value in the prospecting meeting through the use of TCs, a sales game changer. How to do this through improving an important aspect of your target's business.

You now have all the information you need for prospecting with impact!

CHAPTER 3: PROSPECTING WITH IMPACT

In this chapter, we review effective approaches to get in front of your prospects and why your personal brand is equally as important as the company's brand.

We remember things such as events, people, places and cultures that have a big impact on us; they stand out in our mind. We can recall them quickly as they've made a lasting impression. Creating an impression from your prospecting call may seem like a tall order, but now you have all the ammunition you need to do just that.

From your company and sector insights, you have the seeds of an idea for a TC and you've considered how your company could develop a solution for that. Now you want to get it in front of your target companies.

Before you start prospecting, it's important that you get yourself in the right mental state for prospecting success. This means feeling positive and unstoppable, so it comes across in your voice. If you make calls when you feel stressed, anxious or down, you won't achieve high performance and success. It will prevent you from achieving your potential and waste time in the process.

At this juncture, you are keen to meet your prospect and to tell them about your TC as it has the potential to make a real difference to their business. Through your insights you have information to be enthusiastic about, let that shine through!

Success Tip

Here are some ways to get into a positive frame of mind before you start prospecting:

1. Listen to, watch or read something that inspires you. This could be music, a personal development video, quotes or an extract from a book.

2. Think of a time when you were very successful; remember how you felt at that time. Recall details such as what you wore, where you were, how you spoke, stood and behaved. Re-live that moment and feel the success.

3. Hold on to that feeling as you start the prospecting calls. Create a vision of success for the calls, such as a specific number of qualified appointments made in a certain time frame.

If you've not tried ideas like this before, don't dismiss them. Give them a go and see how they improve your performance. Don't rush the process, put 10-15 minutes into these techniques and if necessary, repeat them if you feel your motivation or enthusiasm dipping.

Having a mindset for success makes a substantial difference to your performance.

The powerful prospecting combination

There are a myriad of business to business prospecting methods. The ones I've included here are the ones that I've had the most success with and that have worked well in other organisations. If you have your methods that work well, use those or combine them with some of these ideas and then compare the results.

These prospecting techniques combine digital and physical approaches. As you would expect, it builds on the insights you've researched.

Social Media

Connect with your prospect on social media, using the most relevant platform. LinkedIn is currently the one for businesspeople. Have a good reason (not a sales one) as to why you would like to connect with them. Personalise your message to connect. This could be mentioning that you've read an interesting article about a project they are undertaking, saying it caught your attention and you'd like to connect. Or the company has recently announced good results in a market that's taken a battering and you're interested to know how they've achieved it and say congratulations (you already have a lot of this information from your research).

Other than your main target contact, consider who else might be involved in the decision-making process to select a new supplier. At the first meeting you can ask your contact who they might be and connect with them either with a quick introductory email or via social media. The larger the business, the more people are likely to be involved in the selection and decision-making process; you need to get to know them.

When they connect with you, do not follow up with a sales message; there is no quicker way to alienate your new connection. Instead read and comment on their posts to gain further insights.

Phone and Email

If you have their contact details (they might show these on their LinkedIn profile), give them a call or email to say, "We've just connected on LinkedIn and we're keen to get your opinion on a new report/white paper/sector insights report that our company has researched. It shows companies how to deal with the growing challenge of (list a relevant challenge) which many companies in your sector are concerned about"

Depending on their response, it could lead to a meeting, video call or webinar to take them through your insights. It doesn't matter if you don't have a big white paper to take them through, you have the insights from your research which you can put into a presentation, along with your ideas for a TC. Aim to take them through the report rather than send it to them. If they insist on it being sent, send a highlights version and agree on a follow-up call in a couple of days to get their view on that first.

Agreeing to this gives you a good reason to call them back, it starts to build trust that you do what you say. As they've agreed it allows you to be more persistent in your follow up. Unfortunately, it doesn't guarantee that they'll be available or even take your call, but don't give up on the first attempt.

Personalised Letter

If all best attempts to contact your prospect by phone failed and you've not been able to speak with them, send instead a personalised letter. Keep it short and to the point. You know from your research what they are trying to achieve and your TC idea has the potential to make an important difference to their business. In this time of online communication a physical letter stands out, especially one that shows you have an understanding of their business.

In your letter you are enticing them to engage with you; they have nothing to lose, except 20 minutes of their time for you to present your findings. At the end of the letter say that you will follow up with a call next week to discuss it further and get their feedback.

In the resources section at the back of this book you will find Template 4 – a personalised letter, which you can tailor to your target company.

My own rule of thumb is that I aim for at least five or six attempts using different approaches to make contact across social media, phone, a personalised letter and email. Check if any of your contacts can refer you. If all of this fails to raise any response or interest, then I accept it for the time being. It's not actually a no, which means it could be yes at some future point. Keep them on the list and try again in a few months.

I've waited over a year for a target prospecting meeting. During that time, I kept in touch and increased my knowledge of their sector. When I was invited to meet the executive team my product had improved, my insights were more detailed and it was one of my best prospecting meetings.

 Success Tip

If the receptionist won't give out the email address or mobile number of the person you want to speak with, it never ceases to amaze me how easy it is to overcome this. If you call a branch, shop, or different office of the company and ask for the contact details they are often given to you.

Another option is to call their sales team. Explain that you're facing one of those sales challenges, which no doubt they too will have faced and could they tell you who the contact is and the best way get in touch with them – this works so well!

The phone remains one of the most cost-effective prospecting methods because you can make a good number of calls in a day and the cost is lower than alternatives. When you have cold prospects to contact who don't know you or your company, it reduces your conversion ratios. Take that into account and don't be disheartened by a lower response rate. After a while, you will know how many calls you have to make to get interest.

How to structure your prospecting phone call

Winning big accounts requires a different approach to selling. You're building a relationship and adding strategic value that will unlock a problem that your prospect might not even have identified.

I don't think anyone is really pleased to receive a prospecting call. They are an unplanned interruption, so it's best to get to the point quickly and demonstrate that you have something of value to discuss with them.

Prospecting telephone call structure

1. State your name and company name.
2. Thank them for taking the call.
3. Say what your company does; keep it succinct.
4. State the reason for your call – this is where you talk briefly about one or two of the most interesting insights you have into their sector. Say that you'd like to find a convenient time to discuss it further with them and to share how these insights could make a difference to their business. You could add how impactful it could be, especially as their business is growing, or recruiting or other relevant points that you have discovered in your research.
5. Confirm that they are the right person to speak to on this topic. If not, who would they suggest you speak to? You are likely to have the correct person from your research, but it's worth checking.
6. Say you only need 10-15 minutes for further discussion and suggest some dates.

I am often asked if, when you are put through to your contact, it's best to ask if the prospect has time to take the call or offer to schedule a call for another time.

My view is that if you've got them on the phone and thanked them for taking the call, you should continue. If they say it's not convenient, accept that, don't push it any further and ask for a convenient time.

If you ask if it's a good time and they say no, you've lost your chance as you may not get hold of them again. Strike while the iron is hot, respect their decision if, unprompted by you, they say that it's not a good time.

Success Tip

Remember at this stage of the sales cycle the approach is about positioning you, your business and your expertise by sharing relevant insights that will help the prospect achieve their strategic goals or business drivers.

On the call it is important that your message includes the following points:

- You briefly mention other companies in their sector that you work for and what you have achieved for them. This gives a level of credibility and trust.
- You demonstrate your knowledge of their business and the sector. This builds credibility.

    Include some highlights from your insights research, checking that they resonate with them on the call and say that you'd like to discuss your ideas and TC to overcome or develop these points into a way forward. Add that you consider it has the potential to add value to their business strategy.

Prospecting call example

"Thank you for taking my call Ted, my name is Simon and I represent A2 Media. We provide marketing solutions that increase brand awareness of businesses through PR and social media. We've done this for xyz companies in your sector and achieved a 30 percent increase in engagement and lead generation in three months. Recently we undertook research into lead generation methods and trends in your sector and it gave us some illuminating insights into how it can be further improved. I'd welcome the opportunity to share these with you, as well as the impact it will have on companies who aren't planning for these trends. I believe it could be useful to your business because of your growth plans. I understand this is your area of responsibility?" (Pause for their reply)

Using this approach sets you apart from other prospecting calls because you're sharing a snippet of valuable information about your research which will attract their attention and pique their curiosity. If there is hesitancy or you sense resistance, follow up with:

"I would appreciate just ten to fifteen minutes and if I haven't added value to you in that time then I will happily leave a copy of the insights report/presentation as a thank you for your time and not delay you any further (pause), that's fair isn't it?"

This is how you could respond to a "No".

"Thank you for your response, who do you think would be interested in looking into the sector trends? Maybe a colleague or a member of the Executive Team?"

You could mention a couple of names that you've looked up, or if they mention a name ask for their contact details. If the conversation is going well, could they introduce you?

You may think that I have missed out qualifying your prospect, but you have already completed the research to know that the company is right for your business to target. It is important to check the contact can make or influence a decision at a senior level.

Scheduling prospecting

Put aside fifty-minute blocks for prospecting phone calls. Then take a ten-minute break. Get up, walk around, then get back to it. Make sure you're not distracted. Every interruption costs time as it breaks your thought pattern and it takes time getting back into the swing of it.

Consistent prospecting pays off. You have to take action every day to have a strong pipeline of opportunities, by making connections with new targets. Understand your conversion ratio at each stage of the sales process. It will enable you to predict how many sales calls you need to make to gain a meeting and what your conversion ratio is from meeting to opportunity.

Trade association or professional bodies for prospecting

Collect details of the professional bodies that your targets are members of. Go to their websites and look at the events they are holding and topics being discussed. Consider how your insights and ideas are relevant and add value to current topics. Further develop the ideas being discussed or provide a different perspective. Contact the organisation and offer to write an article for their website. Explain how and why your information would be beneficial to members and how sharing them would add value. Here are some other ideas to reach your targets and position your expertise.

- Provide a free webinar for members – a good way to get engagement and feedback on your insights.
- Provide content for their newsletter. This would need to have a call to action at the end of the article that enables you to get their contact details, such as to sign up for a webinar, an event, or report.
- Offer a reduced cost trial of an element of your product or service.

All of the above approaches have the potential for you to engage with companies that are your targets. This is just the beginning, the very early stages of creating a sales funnel. Take them on a journey to engage with your company multiple times to build trust. In my experience it takes between 6-15 touchpoints from initial contact to winning the business.

Here are some ways to increase the number of touchpoints after the initial contact:

- Send a pdf of your talk or highlights from your insights and TC
- Invite them to a webinar or event
- Offer a one to one consultation
- Invite them to see your operation
- Connect on social media
- Send a brochure, case studies or articles

Success Tip

Take action! You have the details of the professional bodies and trade associations through your earlier research. Get in touch to discuss your ideas about how you can add value to members.

Referrals

A good referral saves your time and takes you straight to a pre-warmed up conversation with your prospect. Building a team of referrers that regularly send you leads is well established in some sectors. For example, law firms get referrals from Banks and Financial Advisors, enjoying a steady stream of leads from them. If you don't currently have a referral network think of three groups that could potentially refer leads and work to you. For example, for a business that provides investment to growing businesses, their three referral groups could be business consultants, accountants and tax advisors.

Select one of those groups to focus on to start with so they get to know you and vice versa. This way trust is established and they can refer you with confidence and knowledge of your business.

A more immediate way to get referrals is to ask your contacts, clients and employees. This is easier with your list of targeted companies as you can be specific when asking if they know these companies and anyone who works there. You could do the research in advance and see if any of your contacts are connected to your targets on social media.

A quality referral is when your referrer 'sells' you into the company you want to meet. To do that you will need to help your referrer by giving them some key reasons why the target should meet with you. Think how you can help your referrer make the intro. Provide a short summary with a few bullet points that link to your insights, such as sector trends presented in an infographic.

A surprising example of how this works is in an accountancy firm that provides events for other accountants in the area. At first glance this seems odd, why would you want to host events for your competitors? As it turns out the other accountancy companies are smaller and often unable to undertake all the work they get. To overcome this they refer it to bigger companies they have a relationship with, who they know have the resources and reputation to do a good job.

A summary of the referral process:

1. Look through your network of contacts that you know well enough to ask for a referral, include your existing clients. Ask them if they know anyone who works in one of your target companies or the actual person you'd like to meet. If not, ask them if they have a contact in the sector you are targeting, who might be able to help you.
2. Send your contact a brief, outlining your insights and why you think it would be of interest to the target so that they can make an informed introduction.
3. If you offer a referral fee explain that to your contact. If not, offer to reciprocate and ask how you could help them with a return favour.
4. Ask your contact to get in touch with your target person and explain why it would be beneficial for them to speak with you. If they agree, the door is open; follow up quickly and make your introduction with a view to discussing your insights with them.

Brand and congruency

As soon as you connect with an individual on LinkedIn or via a phone call, they're probably going to check out your profile online. Your personal brand is as important, if not more so than your company brand.

Why? Because although you represent the business, you are the person they will build the relationship with.

The impression you create matters. Will what they discover be a good representation of you? Does your profile show what you stand for, your values and how you work with businesses in their sector? Does it showcase your experience and knowledge? Or does it just include a list of companies that you've worked for, but not your value and expertise?

Do you appear as an expert in your field? Does your profile picture show you in a professional light, without sunglasses and not at the Christmas party? If you scan LinkedIn looking at profile pictures, you'll be surprised at how unprofessionally some people represent themselves when it can be so easily and inexpensively improved.

Success Tip

Ask a few colleagues to give you their impression of your online profile, ask them to be a critical friend answering the following questions:

Does your profile reflect your expertise?

Does your profile represent you in a professional light?

Does your profile show how you deliver value to companies?

Is your profile congruent to the brand of the business you represent?

Consider their feedback and act upon making improvements.

Here is a checklist of do's & don'ts for making a good impression on LinkedIn.

Do:

- Use a professional head shot.
- Complete your contact information.
- Make it clear how you add value in your intro, rather than what you do. Change, 'I'm a business development manager for PT Software' to 'I enable businesses to understand and use the best cloud software that improves efficiencies by up to 40 percent in their company'.

- Make sure email notifications are turned on, then respond promptly to messages.
- Keep your profile current and complete.
- Set the settings on your LinkedIn profile to your preferences. For example, in the privacy settings where you have options such as to view contacts without them knowing.
- After connecting, you could ask if they be interested in receiving some sector highlights about trends and challenges. Avoid going straight to offering your product or service.
- Have some endorsements on your profile. Ask clients or colleagues for them as this builds your credibility.
- Like and comment on other people's posts, show engagement, especially with your targets.
- Post content, preferably your own, that is relevant to your targets.
- Consider sending a note to ask if you can help when someone relevant views your profile.

Don't:

- Ever bad mouth a company, individual or group.
- Connect with people you don't know without a personalised message.
- Make your first message or even your second one a message to buy your products. Basic I know, but it still happens!
- Ignore messages, be responsive.

Prospects are also likely to check out your company website and that needs to be congruent with your messaging. Take time to review your company website from the perspective of a prospect and ask yourself if it aligns with your pitch and what messages would prospects get.

If it's not aligned, what can be changed? Add a blog post from you that relates to your insights. Include your contact details and a call to action at the end of the blog post, such as fill out the form to receive a more detailed report. If you work with the marketing department, find ways to use the website to build trust and engagement with prospects and support the development of your sales funnel. This could be a questionnaire or scorecards which encourage engagement, or relevant sector insights and reports they can download. Review your other marketing collateral such as brochures and banners. Cast a critical eye over them, are they representative and supportive of your sales message? If not, create new ones and include interesting points from your insights.

When prospects sign up for webinars and events ran by the marketing department, be sure that the marketing team notify you. They are prospects and you must follow up with them afterwards to see what they thought about the webinar and what interested them about it. This allows you to develop the conversation and potentially move them into the sales funnel.

There is software available that can inform you which companies have looked at your website. This is useful information that shows if your prospects are beginning to engage with your company, especially following a marketing initiative or prospecting call.

To summarise - in this chapter we've covered:

- How to use social media to connect with your prospects and how to approach them without driving them away.
- Using a personalised letter to supplement your prospecting.
- How to structure your prospecting phone call with impact using insights to get their attention.
- The referral method for meeting prospects.
- The importance of your personal brand.

Now the exciting part- successful prospecting meetings!

CHAPTER 4: SUCCESSFUL PROSPECTING MEETINGS

In this chapter I detail how to use your researched insights to develop conversations with your top twenty to thirty target prospects, along with techniques to turn those conversations into exciting new business opportunities.

The prospecting meeting is your opportunity to combine your sector and company insights with your sales skills. It is a good environment to build trust and overcome objections. In your prospecting meeting, your objective is to persuade your prospect that your company has the ability to help them achieve a transformation that is aligned to their business drivers or strategic goals. This might be to show them how future challenges or trends will impact their business, which your company has the skills to help them overcome. This chapter details how you do this.

Presenting your ideas

Your marketing team may arm you with material to help you in the prospecting process. Not generic company information, but relevant to the sectors you are targeting. This can be very useful, but if that's not the case, you can still make progress without it; it doesn't have to hold you back at all.

Consider the marketing literature to be an extra tool in your kit box. Nice to have to reinforce your insights and messaging, but you can still do a great job without it.

Be clear of and understand your company's competitive advantage and factor that into your meeting.

According to management guru Michael Porter the sources of competitive advantage are:

- Costs – providing the same service with less cost than competitors. An example of this is budget hotels and airlines.
- Differentiation – higher price than competitors through a differentiation that client's value. An example of this is luxury holidays or designer products.

Through your insights research, you will know the sector well enabling you to present useful and relevant ideas to your prospects. Additional evidence to support your insights in the form of secondary research, case studies or market trends analysis will further enhance your presentation. Successful salespeople know that the prospecting meeting is crucial in convincing the prospect to progress to the next stage. They've already shown an interest in your company by agreeing to meet, demonstrating that they want to find out more. Now you need to explain how it will be of value to their business

Qualifying your target

As a salesperson, you have a responsibility to use your time wisely and not waste it. Your time is an expensive resource and while converting every prospect isn't realistic, making sure you have a qualification criterion for prospects is important. The benefit of the insights research is that you have pre-qualified the companies you are targeting and checked that you have the right contact.

A qualified target is:

1. A company that you have researched that meets your selection criteria as detailed in chapter one and two.

2. An individual in that company who can either influence a decision at a senior level or is a decision maker.

You will note that I haven't said that they are interested in your product or service. Your role in the meeting is to show them that they need your offering because of the TC you are presenting. At this point they might not realise they need it, for example knowing how a future trend may impact their business.

Success Tip

Attend the prospecting meeting with clear outcomes of what you want to achieve from it and how it could happen.

This first meeting is not about discussing cost or terms; it's a value exchange. Its purpose is for both you and the prospect to establish that there is merit in progressing the discussion further because of a genuine interest.

At the meeting, you both establish that there is an opportunity worthy of investing more time and resource in. You introduce your TC, discuss it and ask how high a priority achieving it would be to them. You also use the meeting to build rapport and to demonstrate that you are knowledgeable in their sector. That you have interesting and relevant insights and ideas that can make a positive difference to their business.

Preparing for the prospecting meeting

Show your prospect something new and thought-provoking from your insights; your aim is to add value and be impactful.

Consider their potential objections and have some responses prepared.

Think about the questions you will ask to develop rapport with your prospect, such as how long they have been with the business, hobbies or recent holidays. Explain that you have researched and know their company's top priorities and ask how they impact the prospect's short and medium-term strategy. Encourage them to engage by asking open-ended questions and making them feel relaxed and comfortable with you.

No objections, no questions, no win

If you're not getting objections or questions about your insights or TC, it's unlikely you'll win business or progress to the next stage of the sales process. Objections and questions are the prospect's way of gaining clarity and understanding. It shows that they are engaged.

If your prospect doesn't seem willing to come up with objections or questions, it shows a lack of interest. Objections are also a good opportunity for you to demonstrate your depth of knowledge in their business and its sector. In turn, this enables you to discuss the benefits of your TC and how it overcomes their concerns and objections.

How to handle objections

Getting into the objection is important and it always has to be taken seriously. You need to understand why the objection has been raised and what is behind it. Often the objection is a lack of understanding and gives you a chance to provide more information.

Using probing questions is the best way to unravel an objection and get to the heart of it. Don't ignore the objection; it is your gift. Unwrap it with enthusiasm, as good things will be revealed.

First, acknowledge their objection; you don't have to agree with it, but it shows you are listening. Take it on board and consider it. Don't brush it under the carpet and ignore it, as this approach may frustrate your prospect and put an end to the discussion.

To investigate the objection, use statements such as:

- I'm really interested to know why you think that because we have customers who had a similar view to that at the beginning. When we got a more in-depth understanding of their situation, we were able to show them a cost-effective way to overcome it.
- I'm keen to understand the reason for that in more detail. Your situation sounds different and it will help us both to know if we *can* add value to your business.

Remember how you say it is as important as what you say. Show interest; you really do want to understand more. Be inquisitive, not accusative or aggressive and avoid the condescending 'we know best' attitude.

Here is an example of objection handling

This sales conversation took place on a video conference call where I was presenting a sales development programme and some objections were being raised.

First objection:

Prospect: "We already have a development initiative in the business, which we've just signed off and I think what you're offering clashes with that."

My response: "I agree, it wouldn't make sense to duplicate training. Could you be specific about where you think the clashes might be please, so I can confirm if it does in fact clash with our programme?"

This gave me the chance to see if the prospect's assumption was actually correct. If it was, I would have said so and suggested changing that part of the programme. As it turned out that wasn't the case and I was able to clarify that. (This response may well have surprised the prospect, here was a salesperson prepared to say it might not be a good fit rather than continue to push for a sale.)

Second objection:

Prospect: "We would have to bring our colleagues in from other countries to attend and that will increase costs."

You can see their engagement here as they are beginning to think about the implications of going ahead with the training.

My response: "When they come across for other meetings, perhaps we can tie the training in with that in order to keep travel costs and time to a minimum?"

Notice key points in the example:

1. The objection is acknowledged.
2. Establishing if the product was actually the same as being offered by asking questions.
3. Overcoming objections by suggesting a way forward.

It's always a good idea to have prepared responses to common objections such as the timing isn't right, we don't have a need, the price is too high or I'm not the decision-maker (which won't be the case with you because you have pre-qualified them).

It's important to understand the real reason behind these objections, which could be fear of change, it's too much effort to change, or they don't like your product or aspects of it.

Use a child's game

Have you ever played the game with young children when they ask you something and you reply with a why, then they answer and you ask why again and keep asking why to each response?

It can be fun to see how they react and think as you delve deeper. The same principle applies when you want to understand a statement or objection that your prospect has made that you need to understand what is behind it. Probe into it, but use a more sophisticated response than *why* each time. Delve down three to four layers if needed, but always bring it back up to a high as otherwise it can feel like an investigation.

Using analogies to illustrate your points

Analogies are effective because they are easier for us to relate to. Let's take a common objection: "I haven't got the time for it; it takes too long and we're really busy."

Response: "That's similar to most of our clients, (acknowledge the objection) who don't have time either. We have a bespoke solution that takes this into account and still delivers results. This is comparable to getting fit; if you don't get started you won't get any results. However, with an instructor tailoring a programme specifically for you, you will achieve your goals quicker and won't be wasting time on the wrong type of exercise.

That's why we tailor the solution for companies in your situation; you get results quicker than doing it yourself without a specific plan. Our process is proven to be very effective within eight weeks, taking less than an hour a day of your team's time for implementation."

Prospecting meeting structure

The structure for the prospecting meeting is next. This is where you present your sector insights and TC, to build traction and engagement. It requires you to have undertaken the pre-prospecting preparation outlined in previous chapters. This preparation is your foundation for more effective selling and winning big. The analogy of building your home on firm foundations for it to last and weather storms, applies here. If you miss out the pre-prospecting work, your transformational sales approach will collapse!

Sharing your insights enables you to engage in a more progressive conversation. This will build engagement faster, by showing your prospect information that will be of interest to them early in the meeting. You already know so much about your prospect, you don't have to waste their time with basic questions about their business.

In addition, you come across as someone who already has an interesting perspective. It's worth the prospect's precious time to find out how your expertise can benefit their business.

Be an influencer - enter the meeting with the mindset of being an influencer or consultant, with useful new insights that will help the prospect achieve their vision and goals faster or more effectively.

Value exchange - following introductions, present your sector insights and TC (which might still be a seed of an idea at this stage), which link to improving their business drivers and strategic goals.

Ask questions as you go through your insights to gather their feedback, opinions and views. Remember that this meeting is a value exchange. If they don't agree with what you are presenting, ask why; what is their perspective or experience (using the objection handling techniques covered earlier)?

Gain confirmation that your insights add value or show a different and useful perspective which is relevant and pertinent to the prospect's business, goals and aspirations. Have case studies to show proof of how your company has made a big difference to other clients.

Showcase your knowledge - reiterating your knowledge of the prospect's business and their sector creates impact and builds confidence and trust in you. For example you could say, "Having read xyz article from your company, I know that lowering the cost of recruitment by getting the right fit of candidates is important to you and the company.

Our approach increases fit factor with our pre-interview online assessment, based on an individual's work preferences. We also know that the recruitment pool has decreased by over 12 percent in the last 6 months, which must be making recruitment costly and challenging to your business. Our approach overcomes this problem." (If the article you refer to has come from a senior representative of the business, it will be a hard one for the prospect to ignore!)

Measure the impact - if you were to deliver the new TC in their business, ask how big an impact it would have on them and their business results. Link this to their business drivers which you researched in the pre-prospecting process. This could be utilisation, market share and/or occupancy levels.

Asking this question about impact is advantageous because it makes the prospect think about their responsibility to do what is right for the business and its goals and objectives. Wait for their response before you go any further and if that means a bit of silence, stay with it.

If the impact isn't big, use probing questions to find out why. You need to establish why the prospect considers the impact to be insignificant. Explore the validity of their response. Is there a rationale? Is there something more significant to them? Ask questions until you find the answer to what that would be.

When you've established what it is, ask them what impact it would have on them personally and then on their team. This will start to give them the all important emotional buy-in as they envisage that.

When they have answered what would make a big impact to the business and to them, you have valuable information. You also know the downside of that impact not materialising, both of which are extremely useful pieces of information in progressing the opportunity.

Understand the barriers - should the impact be worthwhile and beneficial, then it is important to openly discuss what barriers would have to be overcome to deliver it. Jointly work through each of those barriers to discover options to overcome them.

Reassure your prospect that other companies you work with had similar situations (only if that is the case) and this is what you did to remove them. As you jointly consider ways to overcome the problems, agree the top three approaches and confirm why they are the best options.

Others involved – establish who else will be involved in the decision-making process and what their role will be.

Confirm next steps - agree on the best way to progress the opportunity or TC further and take it to the next stage. This could be:

- Inviting them to see your operation
- Preparing a proposal
- Meeting other decision-makers in the prospect's business to present your insights and TCs.
- To send copies of your presentation both in digital and physical format for your contact to use when discussing it later with others involved in the decision-making process.

I prefer to send the presentation afterwards. You may want to update the presentation in light of new information gained from the meeting. Agree timelines and most importantly…

Follow through on what has been agreed – This builds trust, which is a vital ingredient throughout the sales process.

Success Tip

In the meeting, you don't detail *how* you will put the transformational concept into place. You're not giving that away at this stage and you might not have all the details to be able to do that anyway.

You are selling a concept that you know your company has the ability to deliver, even if how you do this hasn't yet been defined.

Preparation is power

By now you will appreciate that through the pre-prospecting process preparation is essential, but for good measure here's another example.

Can you over prepare?

I had an appointment which I had patiently waited 6 months for. When the time came, we had an initial video conference call that went well and we arranged another meeting.

The preparation for the meeting took time because it was a big opportunity and I wanted the presentation to offer some very different insights and concepts.

The interesting point came when I presented the 10-page detailed insights document and TC. At page 4 the prospect said, "Ok, you've covered everything I wanted to get from this meeting, now let's talk about how we make it happen!" In theory, I needn't have spent the time working on it, but the confidence that the research and insights gave me enabled me to be relevant, introduce innovation and be effective in the meeting.

Never underestimate the power of pre prospecting preparation!

Building trust to move your opportunity forward

It goes without saying that building trust is one of the cornerstones of a strong relationship. Trust takes time to build through consistent reliable responses, action and behaviour. So how can you build trust more quickly?

Here is a list of ways to do that and as small as they may seem, they begin to position you as a trustworthy person. With trust, you have influence and your perspective is taken seriously.

Ten ways to quickly build trust

1. Do what you say you will do. This sounds so simple, but just in doing that you will stand out! Follow up, phone back, respond when you say you will. I am constantly surprised by how few people do this.
2. After the meeting, send a thank you for their time and list out the actions agreed.

3. Follow through on actions you commit to and let them know you've done them.
4. Remember things they told you, such as holiday, family details and refer to them when you next meet. This not only shows that you listened, but that you took the time to remember and are interested in them as individuals.
5. Listen actively and refer to points previously discussed or mentioned earlier in the meeting. *(Active listening is when you concentrate on what the person is saying, taking into account non-verbal language such as facial expressions and body language.)*
6. Send them articles or podcasts, or even a book on subjects they are interested in. This creates a positive reminder to them of the meeting.
7. Offer to make connections for them that might be useful and follow through.
8. Ask them what else you might be able to help them with. For example, sharing your insights with other members of their team, perhaps as a lunch and learn session.
9. Ask them if they'd like to meet other members of your team or speak with clients of yours. This provides opportunities for them to build trust with your business and their response will give you an insight into their level of interest.
10. Be conscious of your body language and theirs, hold eye contact (but not for long fixed periods, as that's off-putting!) Look for behavioural cues such as fidgeting. Responding to these signals shows that they can rely on you to be relevant to their needs.

You may already know what has been listed, but ask yourself when you last did it and how consistently you apply it? If it's not consistent pick a few from the list and commit to implementing them at your next meeting. The more trust you build, the more your chances of success increase considerably.

Your follow-through builds trust and I know I've said it previously, but it still stuns me how companies and their representatives don't keep their promise. Recently I was interested in finding out about attending a two-day conference. I wanted to know more about the opportunity of hosting one of the meals with prospects attending the conference.

A time and date were agreed with the conference organiser to have a more detailed conversation about it. We even had a calendar invite, so it was in both of our diaries. At the allotted time, I called him and left a message saying I was free and would await his call. Half an hour passed with no ring back and no email. I emailed him to say it was a shame he didn't make the call. If he had responded that day and apologised, I would have had some empathy with that; it happens, things crop up. He called back a week later with a poor excuse…it was a week too late; any trust had evaporated!

Do's and Don'ts when presenting your ideas at the prospecting meeting.

Do

- Refer to articles you've read about your prospect's future company developments and how your TC could make that happen faster, more effectively and efficiently.
- Look for signals that confirm what you are saying resonates with your prospect. This could be asking questions, concentrating on what you are saying, not being distracted, or a leaning in body position.
- Ask questions to validate your insights.
- Build rapport and make an emotional connection with your prospect, such as how you would improve their results, position and/or performance. Then ask (and this is important for emotional buy-in) how pleased their colleagues, team and leader would be about achieving the results? How pleased would they be if your TC and solution made life easier for them?
- This technique helps your prospect to create some visualised images and feelings about the impact of the results and become emotionally connected to them. You will know their level of engagement from the questions they ask and their participation in this process.
- Get buy-in by asking for feedback as you are presenting, don't wait until the end of the presentation. A note of caution, if your prospect is a talker, keep a check on time and stay on track. You have content to get through and a time to finish the meeting!
- Talk about the impact that the TC could have on their business. If they ignore the insights and trends you are presenting to them, talk through the negative impact of not responding to them. This could be less revenue, higher costs or increased staff turnover for example. Scarcity and lack might be more of a motivator for them. For example when we are in a store and someone picks up the last of something that object becomes instantly more appealing!

- Establish what motivates them to make progress, is it fear of being left behind or excitement about a new future? Tailor your approach accordingly.
- Showcase examples of other companies in their sector who have benefitted from working with your company. This provides credibility.
- Talk through what worked well, lessons learned and how you made improvements. This may help to overcome concerns they have that they aren't voicing.
- Follow up promptly with an email thanking them for their time and notes on what was discussed and agreed.
- Include points that will resonate and excite other executives from different disciplines involved in the decision-making process.

Don't

- Start by presenting your company, what you do and how you do it. Instead grab their attention by talking about their sector and the relevant insights you've gained.
- Be dis-interested in what your prospect is telling you.
- Over embellish the results achieved with other clients.
- Underestimate the challenges in achieving the outcomes. Big results take time and reality is valued over unrealistic timeframes and results. This is unprofessional and can damage your company's reputation and yours.
- Focus on how you will deliver the results; it's the what and when at this stage.

A presentation structure to present your insights and transformational concept

Your presentation is a tool to provoke conversation, interest and questions. Here is a suggested structure for it.

Slide one – Set the scene with background information on the insights you have of their sector. This could be current or future trends, disruptive services or products. Don't start with an introduction to your company as that can come later. You want to capture their attention to demonstrate your knowledge and credibility.

Slide two – Relate these insights to the prospect's company and how it might impact their business drivers or vision, goals, strategy or financials.

Slide three - Outline the cost of not responding to this trend or insight and the negative impact it could have on their business.

Slide four – Reveal your TC that will have a positive impact on an important aspect of their business, its drivers and strategy. Link this to the insights you have presented, reversing out the negative aspect of slide three.

Slide five – Use case studies to provide evidence of how you have helped other companies in their sector to improve results and performance. Note: your examples may not be the same as the TC, that's ok.

You are emphasising the principle that you deliver results, that your approach works and that you have the resources and expertise. Talk through the barriers that you had to overcome and see if any of these resonate with your client and the challenges that they face. This will help them feel confident about your company's abilities. Discuss how you would work together to overcome them.

Slide six – Provide details of your company and your relevant products, culture, vision, values, awards, reviews and testimonials.

Slide seven – Summarise key points of your presentation.

Slide eight – List out three or four next steps to progress the opportunity.

As you guide your prospect through the sales process, keep in mind what got you to this place. It was your depth of knowledge of the sector, your preparation, insights and TC that got them engaged, as well as your sales skills and determination. If at this point the prospect is interested in your product and keen to move it forward, you could be well on the way to winning a new client - an exciting moment. However you can't celebrate just yet, there is more to do!

Timescales

The length of time it takes between having a successful prospecting meeting through to winning a big account will vary depending on many factors. Factors such as the scale of the investment, current contractual commitments, legal considerations, corporate sign off and number of people involved in the decision-making process.

The larger the prospect's business and the size of the opportunity, the more executives will be involved in the decision-making process. Over the last few years, I have noticed that number increase with executives across different geographical territories and departments having a part in the decision.

This may cause the decision making process to take longer than expected to conclude, don't get disheartened if it drags on. Persistence pays off; continue to add value to your prospect and increase your sector knowledge. These are the ongoing building blocks to winning then retaining clients for many years.

Sharing your sector insights with a wider audience at the prospect's company will increase your reach. It will also help to position you and your company as one that adds value and influence, is interested and knowledgeable about their company and sector. You can go a step further by inviting influential contacts from the target company to an insights event.

If you arrange an event, invite your existing clients too, as they will do the selling for you! The time between now and the decision-making process should be used to continue to influence the company about your insights, TC and the benefits it brings.

Note: this is unless there is a specific request or a 'closed' period not to contact the decision-makers in that period. In that situation, ongoing influencing can be conducted indirectly with articles and content relevant to the sector and your product offering, which may be seen by the prospect's decision-making team.

For example

Your opportunity is to supply a number of regional hospitals with chemical-free cleaning products.

In the news, there is a breakout of a new strain of virus. This is a good opportunity for you to state how your new antibacterial soaps prevent the transfer of this new virus. You could get some PR on this, which your prospect might spot.

This is an effective way to continually and positively position you and your company as credible experts. All of this helps because the more touchpoints the prospect company's team has with your business, the more familiar you become to them and the more brand awareness is developed.

To summarise, in this chapter we've covered:

- Advanced strategies for handling objections
- 10 ways to quickly build trust with your prospect
- A step by step approach to your prospecting meeting
- An engaging structure to present your insights that will add value from the start
- Do's and don'ts for successful prospecting meetings

CHAPTER 5: WINNING THE BIG ACCOUNT

Following your successful prospecting meeting comes the next step of entering into more meaningful and detailed discussions; explorations about how you might both work together. This chapter covers techniques to win the big account, the transformational close and why it's so effective. Also, how to handle the tender process and effective techniques for overcoming potential hurdles.

You are now at the point where your hard work has paid off and you are either being invited to tender or provide a quote. Everything you do from this point on has to remain congruent with all you have done to get to this stage. You have to continue to stand out as a company that has the knowledge, skills and expertise to deliver transformational results for your prospect. Take your TC and develop it into a solution that will deliver impressive results.

Your proposal

Include in your proposal the interesting and relevant information that you discovered in your insights research.

Emphasise how your TC will have the potential to improve their key strategic goals or business drivers. These may include the following areas:

1. Client acquisition and retention – increasing sales and new business, growing market share, increasing customer loyalty and longevity. Improving the client experience.
2. Financial - improving financial performance - reducing costs/increasing profitability/improving efficiency/increasing capacity/reducing wastage.
3. Competitive Advantage - development of new products or services, entering new markets and territories.
4. Talent Acquisition - attracting, retaining and developing talent.

Your insights and TC have an important role to play in the tender process, as they will continue to set you apart from your competitors.

Through the value exchange meetings, you will have gathered more information from the prospect. You can use this to refine your TCs and increase their relevance to the company. Now your role is to show how you will do this with the solution you provide.

Invitations to tender or requests for a proposal can be prescriptive in how they want you to respond, often requiring long and detailed responses. In addition to your full response, provide a short summary document to accompany your proposal.

This is not an executive summary, more an executive briefing that illustrates your sector insights. Their relevance demonstrates your knowledge of the sector and highlights why your ideas and concepts will have a transformational impact on their business.

This document is useful for busy leaders who are not fully immersed in the whole sale process, but will find value in a 'light' version of the information which they can quickly digest.

Preparing this will be beneficial to you, because your contact is likely to be discussing your proposal with other team colleagues and their senior management team. You want to ensure that your insights and TCs reach them as they provide credibility. They position you and your company as authoritative and knowledgeable, which will provide reassurance if needed.

Remember that your TC has the potential to make a significant improvement to their business. This sets you apart from competitors who are unlikely to be able to demonstrate this without having put the effort into their own insights research of the company and its sector. Therefore, you have a significant asset and your role is to use it to win the business.

The proposal document

In every company I've been involved in, from FTSE 500 to SMEs, when it comes to meeting a tender response deadline, getting the proposal out is a fraught time.

Information changes at the last minute, senior colleagues want to make amends, or you discover errors in the document. No doubt you can relate to this.

Having a 'solution team' that focus solely on compiling an impressive document and taking full responsibility for its completion is the best way to alleviate the potential stress of this situation.

However, a big caveat comes with that; make sure that it's not so corporate that it misses the very essence of what got you to the proposal stage, being:

- Company insights
- Sector insights
- Prospect value exchange meetings
- The TC
- Development of the TC into a solution

Don't spoil all that effort and work with a corporate tender response that doesn't value or consider any of this information. Remain congruent at every step of the process.

Unboxing

Have you seen videos on YouTube of people unboxing their new phone? Undoing the packaging, lifting the lid to reveal the phone and holding it for the first time?

Apple set the bar with a white box and minimalist look. Consider how your proposal will be 'unboxed' (digitally no doubt). Is it full of text, or does it contain visuals such as infographics?

Is it populated with well-designed case studies? Are there links to videos of your team who will manage the account? Or clients talking about what you've achieved for them?

Is the document pleasing to read and professionally formatted like a brochure or company annual report? It could have a personalised message from the MD or CEO saying how excited they are at the opportunity to work together.

Raising the bar on your tender document gives you another opportunity to stand out. Take advantage of it, as it will be in alignment with your approach so far.

The transformational close

There are many different techniques for closing the sale, such as:

- The assumptive close, which assumes the sale has been concluded.
- The option close – "Do you prefer this one or that one?"
- The suggestion close – "I suggest we deliver the new desks on Monday, does that work for you?"
- The urgency close – "We have limited places available, so we need a decision by tomorrow morning."

These approaches might still have their place somewhere, but they are unsophisticated, outdated and trite. They don't work for winning big accounts. The transformational close seals the deal. This is what we have been building up to!

The essence of the transformational close is that through your insights, you know the strategic and business drivers of the prospect, plus you have an in-depth knowledge of their sector. This information is powerful. It has positioned you and your company as knowledgeable about the market and given you the credibility and opportunity to take you to the next stage.

With the transformational close, you combine the insights knowledge with your TC that progresses the strategic aims and drivers of the company. You show them how your solution will enable the attainment of those aims.

It's compelling and positions your solution high above your competitors who will be focusing on the client's here and now challenges and finding a solution for that.

The transformational approach has a more strategic and holistic view, considering future trends in the market, the performance of the prospect's business, competition and sector development. In taking all this into account, you are able to think differently about which solutions will deliver the best results, now and in the future.

In the transformational close, you create a vision of what you will achieve, how it transforms the business, as well as how you will do it.

Your solution will have a level of intelligence that is far more considered than just responding to current challenges. Yes, you have to address their current situation. However with your insights, you show how your solution takes the future into account and how you can adapt and change for that.

Simply trying to figure out how you help prospects to overcome challenges they face today is a one-dimensional approach. Let's recap the transformational process:

1. Collating insights gleaned from the research into the company and sector.
2. The application of intelligent thought to develop a TC from the insights that are aligned to improving the prospect's key business drivers and/or progressing their strategic goals.
3. Presenting the TC and gathering feedback at a value exchange meeting.
4. The ongoing development of the TC in conjunction with the prospect. Refining it so that it is a compelling solution.

This is powerful. It is a modern strategic approach which doesn't need any hackneyed closing techniques.

The transformational close in summary

The amalgamation of insights, into a TC that aligns with the prospect's strategic goals and or business drivers. This is developed into a compelling proposition, which delivers exceptional value through transformational improvements.

Case Study

Here is a case study that demonstrates all of these elements coming together.

Insights

We had targeted a premium national kitchen manufacturer and retailer and began the process of gathering insights.

We asked our regional managers to visit the target company's showrooms and chat with their staff about the products. Asking questions such as how the product was delivered, what delivery challenges they faced, as well as how things could be better.

This information gave us very useful insights about how their customers found it hard to visualise the volume of product they would receive.

On too many occasions, they wouldn't have enough room for it in their home. It would then have to be returned to the warehouse and await another delivery slot. This resulted in delayed fitting of the kitchen, disappointed customers and in turn disrupted the fitter's schedules.

This process also caused an increase in the level of damaged and lost product, as it was being handled multiple times. This rocketed the level of shortages and damages, especially taps and other expensive fittings.

The company had expansion plans and wanted to be recognised as a leader in both quality products and service offering. The experience of the delivery service wasn't aligned to every other aspect of purchasing a kitchen. For example the care taken to design the kitchen, the impressive showrooms and quality of products.

Transformational concept

By factoring this information into our prospecting meeting, we were able to demonstrate how our solution would transform their full-circle customer care strategy.

We created an innovative white glove delivery service. This included a customer care team who would advise the purchasers of the dimensions and number of boxes they would receive.

A tight delivery window was given that suited the customer and avoided the need for them to wait in all day. A series of phone calls were made leading up to the delivery, to keep the customer advised of delivery time or any delays. Product was unboxed in the room of choice and checked for damages.

Photographs were taken of the product and the customer signed for it. Drivers were trained in customer care, even down to putting on shoe protectors so as not to mark the carpet and how to handle any issues.

Small details, such as letting the customer know that they might be parked outside their house for a few minutes after the delivery had been made, were all part of creating an exceptional client experience.

Our innovative TC dramatically improved an important aspect of their business and we went on to win a substantial multi-million pound contract for their total UK distribution.

The contract increased in value annually as we continued to make improvements towards their strategic goals and business drivers. We provided a home delivery service that was frictionless for their customers. The costs of damages, shortages and fitter's downtime were all reduced.

I later discovered that our transport costs were higher than their previous provider and in the upper quartile compared to our competitors who quoted.

However, our proposal focused on the bigger picture, reducing costs in other areas. It transformed an important aspect of their business that aligned to their strategy, which was highly important to them. This made our overall proposition much more attractive to their business as a whole.

Outcomes

We led the market with a new and innovative service. This was a valuable contract to us and not just from a financial perspective. It extended our expertise and reach in an area of market growth.

It enabled us to win other contracts in home delivery as our reputation and expertise grew. It was both a transformational win and a transformational account for the business.

Had we just focused on moving kitchens from their manufacturing plant to the end-user, we would have delivered a solution, but it wouldn't have been transformational. It's highly unlikely that we would have won, let alone kept the contract for the long term.

 Success Tip

When it comes to providing costs, give choice. Three cost options increase your prospect's choice and gives you an increased chance of being successful. Choose a high, medium and low bid with a variant service offering to support it.

The follow-up

Once your proposal or quotation has been received, it can be tricky to know when to follow up. Especially when the timescale for response isn't outlined in the tender document.

My rule of thumb is to follow up within five working days. This gives time for your proposal to have been read and any initial questions to be collated.

I was in a business where they had tendered for a £1m account; this was the third year of bidding for it. On each occasion, they were in the top three bids but didn't make it to pole position.

This year the team felt they would win it; they knew the prospect better and their proposal was stronger. However, they left it too late to follow up after putting in their response.

When they eventually made the call some three weeks later, they discovered they were £600.00 out on the whole contract compared to the company that had won the work.

The company could have easily matched that price and offered to do so, but it was too late. If the relationship was stronger, using the principles in this book, this situation is unlikely to have arisen. The tendering company would have been aware of the price variance before the final decision was made, as they would have been closer to the prospect.

The supplier would have made it clear to the company awarding the contract that the value proposition was far greater than the £600.00 in question. There were no insights or TCs and it had turned purely into a price pitch.

Never assume that the prospect is going to call you. You have to take full responsibility for following up, even if they have promised to call. If they don't contact you on the day they say they will, then call them later that day. It's taken you a lot of work to get to this stage in the process. The follow-through is as important as all the work you've done so far.

Success Tip

A company was one of two in the final stage of a large contract win and it all looked promising for the supplier. They didn't win it, but it wasn't down to price. A competitor had included one of their c-suite executives in the meeting, which provided an extra level of confidence and comfort to the company awarding the contract. They felt more important to that supplier.

Senior Executives may not be able to attend every meeting, but when in the final stages of a big account win, ask your leadership team to support you. The second-best alternative is for them to follow up the prospect with a phone call after the presentation. It shows interest and commitment and it's also quick and easy to do. It has the added benefit of being able to address any concerns or objections that the prospect has after the meeting.

Dealing with radio silence

What can you do when prospects don't respond to your calls and you've not heard anything back from them?

Hard as this might be, you have to accept that your options are limited, so the best thing to do is to get busy with other prospects in your pipeline.

In over 25 years in business, I've yet to come across any company that made a decision by the date they've stipulated. I've learnt that silence doesn't mean no.

You can easily over-analyse it, questioning if it was priced too low or too high, or thinking that they are progressing with your competitors.

They might be. Alternatively, they may have a key decision-maker away from the business, resulting in the project being put on hold until they're back. My advice is not to focus on it, because you're just guessing and making assumptions. If another week passes and they've still not been in touch, call again. Try early morning or after office hours when they may be less busy and more available to take a call.

If you are still not receiving any response or feedback, here are some ideas:

1. Speak to other contacts in your prospect's business that you have met and see if they can shed any light on why a decision is being delayed. Perhaps the business has other issues that have become a priority. In following the steps found within this book, you will have made contact and built relationships with others involved in the decision-making process. They might be able to help you.
2. Keeping communication open is vital, use other methods such as social media to message them. Continue to send interesting and relevant articles, without bombarding them, or invite them to an industry event that is relevant to them.
3. Issue a short questionnaire as part of your quality process to ask questions about the sales process. For example, how would they rate communication, understanding of their issues, response to questions or quality of the proposal?

When all else fails and so much time has lapsed that it's probable that you have lost it, call and say you'd appreciate a formal feedback session. Add that it would be invaluable to improve for next time.

When you do the groundwork outlined in previous chapters, your likelihood of radio silence is significantly reduced because you have built a relationship, influence, trust and an emotional connection.

All of these help you to keep the communication open, ongoing and informed.

Shortlisted!

You've received the good news: you've been shortlisted! This can mean a few things.

- You share this shortlist equally with others
- You are the front-runner
- You are the only player

What happens next might be a fresh round of discussion on your proposal, a further visit to your business, or conversations with clients of yours to verify your product or service.

Whatever pans out next, be ready for the 'you've been shortlisted' call. Don't let the excitement of the call stop you from gaining ground. Use it to gain useful information such as what they liked most about your proposal, aspects to improve, timescales and next steps.

If you gain just one key message from this book, it's the importance of insights. Through research and quality questions, you gain answers that move you towards your goal of winning a big and valuable account.

Winning and contractual negotiations

You've nearly won it, but first you have to navigate the choppy waters of negotiation.

In larger organisations, you may be negotiating the detail of the contractual aspects with a different team, such as purchasing. How often does the salesperson's heart sink when they hear this?

It doesn't have to spell disaster. Having built a strong relationship with your prospect, they will often help you as you finalise contractual agreements with the purchasing team.

If you are a smaller business and the responsibility of finalising the contract and getting it signed lies with you the salesperson, having to work with a professional purchasing team may not be an exciting prospect.

The client's purchasing team will be very happy about it as they will understand the psychology involved. They know that you are keen to get the deal finalised and move on to your next big opportunity. They might take advantage of that by emphasising the things they want from the deal in exchange for what they think you want, which is to get the deal signed up quickly!

This isn't a book about negotiation strategy, but there are a few really effective techniques to cover because it is part of winning big accounts.

Here are some points to consider in advance of the negotiation meeting. Take time to prepare and think through your priorities using the following questions, to give you clarity of what is and isn't acceptable to you and the business.

1. What is your walk-away point?
2. What might you be prepared to concede and why?
3. What do you want in return for any concessions?
4. What you are not prepared to concede at any price?

Negotiation insights

Insights play a vital role in successful negotiation. Put yourself in the shoes of your prospect and gain insights into their perspective and negotiation position.

Consider what pressure points they might have that will influence their negotiation. Is there a timeframe they have committed to because they have to give notice to the incumbent provider? What might be their fallback position? What are the repercussions to their business if you don't agree?

Aim to get all of their negotiation points out on the table, so you have visibility of everything. Look at the complete picture and seek confirmation that it is all listed. Understand why each point of negotiation is important and ask them to prioritise them.

You will then be clear about what they are looking for. On their list might be items that you can easily concede, but don't concede anything without getting a concession from them. This is the art of negotiation!

The shortest time that it has taken me to win a new valuable account using the methods in this book was three months. That was from gaining the commitment from the prospect and the subsequent letter of intent for a three-year term. That turned out to be the easiest part of the process.

What followed in the negotiation on the contractual terms was one of the most protracted I've had to deal with. At times we wondered if it really was worth the effort and I'm sure this was a tactic being used to wear us down.

There was a constant to and fro between the MD of the supplier who I was working for and the client, to talk through the various contractual changes that were being requested. We seemed to be too far adrift on too many clauses to be able to get the final contractual documents signed.

We didn't foresee that every single clause would be challenged and despite our frustration, this was an important contract to win. It was a good fit for us; it suited our skills and competencies well and it was a new innovative service that we could offer to other businesses.

We would be able to deliver an exceptional client experience. Additionally, it was a good name to have in our portfolio, which would open doors for other opportunities. The challenge was: how were we going to get this contract signed without having to spend more legal costs and executive time on it?

We decided to set out a negotiation strategy and we shared it with the soon to be client. The purpose of it was to provide clarity on what we were prepared to negotiate and what we weren't, the reasons why and to get everything out on the table.

We explained that the cost of further negotiation was going to be in the region of £10,000 when we included everyone's time and legal costs. We were prepared to offer that as a one-off discount to be spread across the three years of the contract, on the basis that we agreed a number of specific clauses and improved payment terms.

We knew that manufacturing cost reduction was a key business driver for the client, which we had discovered in our insights phase. Our offered discount helped with that. In return for our proposed price reduction, we negotiated improved payment terms which we considered to be a valuable concession for us.

In addition to that, we had calculated what the financial cost of delaying the start of the contract would have on our business. This was greater than the discounted figure we offered. Thankfully the contract was signed within days, so we were able to get back to the business of winning our next big account.

As long as you are not compromising your key point of contact, they can be invaluable in helping you in the negotiation process with a purchasing team. In many cases, the prospect has made the decision to go with your company and now they have to hand over the contractual terms to this purchasing team with a remit to secure the best deal.

Remember if that is the case you do have influence. You are the preferred company and the aim of the negotiation is to lock in the best deal. The intention is to work with you; the negotiating team won't be keen to go back to the primary contact and say a deal can't be struck.

When contractual negotiations drag on, it can sap your energy and enthusiasm at a rapid rate. Avoid the pressure to give in to demands. If you have to concede, always ask for a concession in return.

Think creatively of different ways forward, so both parties get what is important to them. Keep reminding your client of the value you are providing and asking them where they don't see that value if they are asking for a price reduction. This gives you the opportunity to go over your value again or find new ways to increase your value.

When you have completed the negotiation and been awarded the contract, it is good to celebrate and reflect on your achievements. Review what went well and what can be improved for your next big win.

 Let's now move to part two on how to grow the account and keep it for the long term.

To summarise - in this chapter we've covered:

- How to make your proposal stand out
- The transformational close and why it's effective
- The follow-up and ways to react to radio silence
- Techniques to avoid losing out on contractual negotiations

PART TWO:
GROWING AND KEEPING BIG ACCOUNTS

CHAPTER 6: A TURNING POINT AND MY BIGGEST BUSINESS LESSON EVER

In this chapter, we focus on how to grow existing clients to achieve transformational results. You will discover which clients are the right ones to develop and how to keep them for many years.

At this juncture, we switch focus to transforming growth in your existing accounts. In smaller businesses, the business development or sales manager may have responsibility for both brand new sales and growing sales with established customers.

In larger companies, it's generally two separate roles. If you are an account manager and have skipped straight to this section, you will have missed a lot of very relevant content from part one of the book. This will be extremely useful in your role as an account manager.

I strongly recommend you read part one to understand the process of insights, value exchange meetings and TCs. If you're a salesperson who doesn't have responsibility for growing existing accounts, I encourage you to read on, as you will pick up new ideas that can be applied in the sales process.

What is covered in this chapter applies to accounts that have gone through the on-boarding process, the account is stable and the client is pleased with what you are doing.

All might seem calm in this situation, but this is a vulnerable phase. It is easy to fall into the trap of thinking all is well and take your eye off the ball. In effect, you have three choices of how you progress the account:

1. Park it – don't do anything from an account management perspective to service the account. If that were your approach you'd expect to see service levels decline and complaints to rise.

2. Keep it ticking over – you can keep the account ticking along maintaining service level agreements, having monthly review meetings but applying little effort into developing it.
3. Drive it – you can drive it forward, exploring ways to transform the account, to grow and develop it into a big strategic valuable account for your business.

In logistics, many outsourced contracts are signed for a minimum three-year term. The activity curve of the outsourced provider can often look like an inverted bell. It is regularly stated that this approach is one of the key reasons for clients changing contractors. Through the transformational process outlined in this section, you will have strategies to keep your customers for many years and avoid this pitfall.

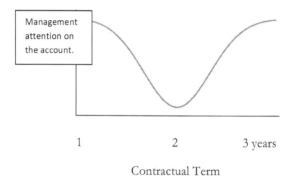

Contractual Term

Fig 1. High activity and focus from the management team at the beginning, low in the middle (year 2) and then it ramps up as the contract comes up for renewal.

About to lose a big account

We won a large account with The Body Shop, a global retailer of cosmetics and body care products. It was such an exciting win for me personally, as it was led by the late Dame Anita Roddick, a highly respected values-driven entrepreneur.

Yet incredibly, I came extremely close to losing it. It was through this experience that the methodology for transformational selling and account management began to emerge. This is the story of how it all started.

It was a murky January morning. I left home early to be at The Body Shop's head office for 9.00 am with a quick stop off for breakfast before a strategic review meeting.

The purpose of the meeting was to analyse performance, especially over the Christmas period. I knew the team had achieved a fantastic set of service standards and I was very confident about the meeting.

We had delivered an outstanding year for them. We had met every difficult key performance indicator (KPI) that had been thrown at us.

We were well prepared and I was looking forward to the team receiving a big pat on the back, including one from Anita Roddick, Founder and Chief Executive.

All was going well in the review meeting until I heard their Supply Chain Director utter the words:

"You're boring. If that doesn't change, we will have to look elsewhere for a new service provider. You've done a great job on achieving all the performance standards, but we'd expect that anyway.

What are you doing that's new, innovative, or different? You're not leading the way, looking at the bigger picture or finding better ways to add value to us. You should be challenging us and coming up with new ideas that will have a positive impact on our business.

Go and think about it and come back to us next month with some ideas."

I remember feebly saying, "But we have a contract." As you might imagine, the response was, "If we have to fall back on that, then we've got an even bigger problem!"

It felt brutal. What more did The Body Shop want from us?

This was such a prestigious contract that was opening up many new opportunities for us to work with other businesses in the retail sector.

The contract had been hard-won and they were my favourite client. Our competitors would be delighted and ready to pounce on the news of us losing this account. If that happened, we'd have a reputation for being inept. Despite the truth of our brilliant delivery performance, what would others believe?

It's often said that from your most challenging moments comes your finest hour. I had no indication or appreciation that this might be the case as I was faced with what I considered to be a most unrealistic and unfair challenge.

I had time to reflect on the drive back to the office. I decided to bring key members of the team together to discuss the situation and see what ideas they might have.

This quickly turned into a brainstorming session, with all the usual parameters. No idea would be mocked; allow ideas to percolate and put your thoughts on post-it notes on the wall.

We had the classic ideas that you would expect from a logistics provider such as improve the KPI's and make them more challenging. I knew that wasn't what The Body Shop wanted; we had to be more creative and think outside of the world of logistics.

The question we kept asking over and over was, what is important to The Body Shop? Somehow, we had to get past saying 'a great distribution service', because that was deemed to be boring! We weren't asking the right questions.

It also felt the wrong way around. Here was the client challenging me, surely it was meant to be the other way around? Weren't we meant to be the experts challenging their approach to logistics and in the process adding value? Isn't that exactly what we'd been doing?

We were, but it was within the confines of logistics. We hadn't thought broader than that; we weren't looking at future trends in retailing or the environmental issues that were so important to The Body Shop.

Our thinking was limited. Although it was hard to swallow, they were right; we were boring. We were focused on logistics, which was limiting our ability to broaden our horizons and become the service partner they wanted. In winning the account, we had put forward and implemented innovative ideas, yet we hadn't continued to do that.

What's more, I had prided myself on our relationship with The Body Shop, but evidently they weren't delighted with us. I had just let the service KPI's speak for themselves as if that was sufficient.

This was when I began to realise that a whole new approach was needed. The Body Shop helped me to formulate a methodology for transformation in key accounts that is as relevant today as it was then. In that threat of losing the business, they had given me a gift.

Following our internal brainstorming session, our fleet engineer had an intriguing idea. His role was to ensure that our fleet of trucks were well maintained and safe. His suggestion was to see if we could create the most environmentally sound truck on the road to do the distribution for The Body Shop.

This sounded exciting. It aligned with Body Shop's broader business principles and values. It was bold, innovative, different and would certainly add impact and value to our service offering to them.

The challenge was, we weren't truck manufacturers and currently all trucks had diesel engines. There was very little research, technology, development, funding or awareness of making trucks environmentally friendly at that time.

We decided to follow through on the idea; it was a bumpy road as truck manufacturer after truck manufacturer turned down the opportunity to work with us on this project.

Each one was saying it couldn't be done. We eventually found a UK truck manufacturer, ERF, who were keen to partner with us on the project.

The Body Shop team loved the idea and we created a joint project with them to develop the concept and see if we could make it a reality. Eighteen months later, a natural gas engine was developed, emitting 25 percent less greenhouse gas.

One of the key problems was that the range of the truck was very limited. There were no natural gas filling stations in the UK, let alone in the vicinity of Littlehampton which was the head office and production centre of The Body Shop. Thankfully Dame Anita Roddick had connections with a local garage owner, who had lent her £4,000 to open her second shop (a successful investment on his behalf) and he was willing to help. The first natural gas refuelling pump was set up in Littlehampton and we were able to go live.

The truck was launched in a blaze of publicity; our relationship with The Body Shop was strengthened and secured. From there on, we built innovation and ways to transform the account into our key performer on objectives and contractual terms. We were never told we were boring again and we kept the account for over fifteen years, yes fifteen years! It grew into another successful and valuable multi-million pound account.

Being close to losing this big account turned out to be one of my most important business lessons. It changed our approach to sales and account management forever. We made sure that transformation and innovation were an integral part of how we did business development.

Selecting the best account for transformation

When you consider all the effort that goes into winning big accounts, it makes complete sense to analyse then maximise the potential they offer for growth. Deciding which ones have the highest probability for transformational growth helps you to determine your priority accounts.

The creation of a Transformational Project (known from here as TP), takes your account to the next level of performance and is something that will benefit your company and your clients considerably.

It can increase account longevity and profitability. It can generate more sales; creating a higher profile of the account in the business and thus ushering in additional resources.

The account manager and team can benefit from both company and client recognition as the ones who transformed the account. This can result in increased trust and opportunities for growth of the business, the account and the individuals involved.

It can also have other unexpected benefits. Imagine being on stage at the company conference because of the success you have had on transforming a key account, talking about how you achieved it. The challenges you and your team overcame, the breakthroughs you had.

This would boost your profile and you would be seen as highly influential. Imagine the same scene, but this time with your client on stage with you, talking about you and the company in a very positive light.

Why stop there? You could attend industry events together talking about what you have achieved. All of which would raise the profile of your company and its capabilities. Other prospect companies might be interested in achieving something similar in their business and call you to discuss it.

As your client already knows you and your company, there is a level of trust in place already. They know the product or service and you have a relationship with them. This makes a good basis from which to take the account to a new level and transform it.

If you have responsibility for a number of accounts, I recommend you prioritise one or two to start with. Take action, deliver results, learn from it and repeat with the next account.

Selection criteria for priority accounts.

The criteria below enables you to decide which are your priority accounts for a TP.

Think about each of your accounts and consider the following statements. Mark them as green for yes, amber for possibly/not sure and red for no.

Criteria for account selection

You can use Template 5 on the resources page at the back of the book to complete the assessment, or it can be downloaded at rjen.co.uk/downloads.

Growth

- Does the account have profitable growth potential?
- Do they have current or future challenges that we could help them with?
- Are there are elements of their work that we aren't doing for them, but could?
- Could we add more value to their business?
- Has the account has grown year on year?

Insights

- Our knowledge of their strategic goals and economic drivers is detailed.
- We know the future trends in their sector and the impact they could have on their business.

Financial

- They are financially sound and they meet our investment /credit status criteria.
- We make an acceptable financial return on the account.

Perception

- They have a positive view of us.

Receptiveness

- They are receptive and open to new ideas and ways of working.

Relationship

- The relationship is strong and positive and they are pleased with what we do for them.

Account selection criteria template

As you work through the account selection questions, you will quickly see which accounts have more green responses and therefore are the more attractive ones to start with.

If you have a lot of amber responses, you don't yet have the level of client detail to make an informed decision as to which account to progress. This means you need to gather the information. Red responses indicate that you either need to gather more information basics or the account has limited opportunity for growth at this stage.

Once you have your two or three priority accounts selected, review the analysis statements with your team and drill into more detail with probing questions. For example; if the account has profitable growth potential ask what is that potential. Is it saleable, what do we need to do to make it happen and how could we make it happen faster?

As you work with the client, you should be able to get this level of detail. If you find that not to be the case, have a strategic insights session with their senior executives and find out what their strategic goals and business drivers are.

You are now already familiar with the concept of transformational change and how to achieve it through sector and company insights. The principles continue in growing your existing accounts, but there are subtle differences. One of the key differences with existing accounts is that you want to have a TP to work on in collaboration with the client as a joint project.

This will be a project that you and the client agree to develop together as a strategic partnership. Before you do that, you need to have a solid relationship on which to build it. If the relationship isn't strong, that needs to be addressed first and there's an excellent approach to help with this detailed in the next chapter.

Once you have completed the account selection questions, bring your team together to brainstorm ideas for a TP. Aim to have at least three ideas per account. Question why your client would be interested in it and how well it links to their corporate strategic drivers. Does it save money, help to grow their business or improve their customer service for example?

Consider how it addresses opportunities and challenges in their sector. What upward trajectory trends, new technologies or market developments are taking place?

Such information will help you when discussing your idea of a TP with your client. The key is that it has to be important to them and enable them to achieve a substantial outcome.

Once you have ideas from the brainstorming session, create a vision of what success with your project would look like. Have your team involved in that process too. Fill that vision with detail, such as how pleased the client will be when the project has been completed. What returns will it generate for both businesses? Will it strengthen the relationship and open up further strategic opportunities?

How one company changed the account from transactional to a strategic partner

A supplier, Taylors, have a business that manufactures personal protection clothing. They supply a client with protective eyewear and safety gloves and want to grow this account.

Richmond, the supplier account executive, had a vision of how he could improve the product and service to his client, but the relationship was transactional and he didn't even know the directors. Many of his ideas to improve the products needed his client to make changes in their operation.

For example, he could offer different products in varying quality levels, giving wider pricing options. This would require the branch assistants to be familiar with the product differentiators and advise their customers accordingly.

He then discovers that sales of one of his top range thermal gloves has dwindled significantly over the last three years. He supplies the same product to other companies and sales had grown substantially.

Richmond went into a number of his client's branches to see if he could find out why. He enquired about the gloves and the store assistants didn't know of them, they had to go to their computer and look them up. He asked about the quality of the gloves, again blank stares from the assistants. No wonder sales had declined.

He decides to create an informational video about the gloves and the different quality levels they came in. The video also outlined the financial returns the gloves could provide to his client. He explains how Taylors would run a training programme onsite for each of the branches so that staff were able to provide the right information to buyers.

Next, he got the contact details of all the directors and sent them each the video in a nicely presented box with a header that said, 'This glove will fit." On the inside of the box it said, "It will also fit your sales and profit goals. It will fit well with your vision to offer a range for every budget. It will also fit your ambition for your store staff to have excellent product knowledge."

A few days later, the purchasing director called him to arrange a meeting. The upshot was, he got a big order and supplied the gloves. From there, he went on to create new products with them because he put a lot of effort into understanding their strategic plans. He transitioned from being a transactional supplier to a respected supplier and partner to the business.

The lesson from this is that you have to consistently be able to add value at a strategic level and to improve a client's business drivers. Understanding this and aligning your TP to achieve this is crucial to gain traction and deliver results for both parties. If you don't know the senior executive team of your clients, it's a priority to get to know them.

Trust and influence

Trust and influence are essential skills to successfully grow an account into a transformational one. The client needs to see you as a person of influence, someone they can trust and whose opinion they value.

From the insights research you have done (detailed in part one) and the knowledge you have of their sector, you will be on your way to being seen as that person. The objective now is to build on that, to grow the account by working jointly with the client on a TP.

Creating the best environment for client transformation

You have selected accounts where the relationship is strong and positive, where there is potential. You now want to set the scene to take it to the next level. This starts with a discussion with your senior account contact about how you would like to work together to increase performance, results and success.

An excellent way to do this is to create a framework that you both agree to. This framework sets a foundation for how you approach problems, overcome challenges and defines the values and vision that you want to achieve.

This framework is separate from the day to day operational KPI's or contractual terms. It's a framework that brings together both of your companies' ethos, culture and values and defines your behaviours. I call this framework a commitment pledge; it becomes the compass for how you work together.

If you involve both your client's and your own team in the process of agreeing a pledge, it increases their engagement and buy-in to the outcomes. Through this process, you will get a good appreciation of the values that are both important and unimportant to your client.

This will prove to be extremely useful in the development of your relationship. When you have agreed on the pledge, it serves as a reminder of your commitment and approach and it should be referred to regularly.

---

5 reasons for having a commitment pledge

1. A reference point of how client and supplier will work together; this establishes what is important for a successful partnership.
2. It can be referred to, to get back on track, should behaviours become out of kilter with the pledge.
3. It creates a culture of trust because both teams know what is important in the relationship and they have a clear framework to operate within.
4. The values in the pledge will influence behaviours; if honesty is stated in the pledge, then it encourages both teams to own up when things go wrong. This means mistakes can be quickly rectified without incrimination.
5. It unites both teams to work collaboratively because everyone is clear about what is expected in working in accordance with the pledge This increases engagement and performance.

Creating and using the commitment pledge

Refer to the commitment pledge at the beginning of each meeting, as a reminder of how you have agreed to interact and prosper together.

Have it on the wall in your office and in theirs. You could all sign it and add in a personalised message of what you will do in support of it.

Refer to it and the importance you give it often; it then becomes the way you do business together.

The pledge comes into its own when you have difficult conversations; the framework helps deal with them. It makes the relationship more collaborative, equal and less adversarial. A good pledge will feel exciting and motivational.

Here is the process of creating a commitment pledge, one that has the buy-in of your team and your clients and which you are all happy to sign up to:

1. Suggest to your client why you would like to have a commitment pledge or charter by outlining the benefits it will bring.
2. If both companies already have defined values, you can use these as your start point. If not, start with the values that are important to you as individuals and use these.
3. Check the values reflect how you want to work together and will enable your relationship to flourish. Words such as openness, trust, integrity, fairness, collaboration might be suitable. When you have a list of between 10 – 20 value words narrow it down to 10 which you jointly agree are the most important ones.
4. Reflect on the final list of words. Will they enable you to achieve what you want to achieve together? For example, if you have chosen passion as a value, is passion going to enable you to develop and transform the relationship? The answer could be yes, but if the words don't feel quite right, take the time to find better ones.
5. With the shortlisted words you have chosen, see if they fit well into your responses to the questions listed next. You could each do this separately and compare your responses and discuss them. Then understand the differences and see how you can align and agree.
6. Write your commitment pledge in the present tense.

Questions to address using the selected value words.

1. Should we make a mistake or an error which causes our client a problem, we commit to handling it with (use the appropriate value words) and vice versa.
2. If you, the client is unhappy with an aspect of our product or service we will (use the appropriate value words).

3. As the client, we commit to speaking and behaving like this (insert phrase using the value words) when we engage with the supplier's team and vice versa.
4. If we have an issue, we commit to addressing it this way (insert words and phrases using the value words).

You can choose other questions that are important to you both and then create a commitment pledge of how you will work together containing the value words that you have agreed.

Example of a supplier client commitment:

"We commit to joint teamwork and equality while driving a passionate and positive attitude towards each other. We'll respect each other's views and opinions and commit to openness and honesty in every interaction. We will be open to new ideas and innovation that delivers value for both businesses.

We will act responsibly and methodically approach challenges with the intention of finding mutually acceptable solutions. Any unacceptable behaviours such as unrealistic demands, lack of respect and fairness, which cannot be resolved by both teams, will be addressed and resolved at a senior level.

We commit to making our relationship between the two companies a beacon of success. This will be an example of what can be achieved when two teams are united behind our big ambition of being the best partnership. Our goal is that both parties renew the contract for decades to come."

Once you have agreed this, create simple measures and examples of acceptable behaviours, so all involved are clear.

To summarise - in this chapter we've covered:

*   A process for analysing the accounts, which will be the best fit for a TP.
*   How to create a culture that will improve the relationship and behaviours between supplier and client teams.
*   How to kick-start a TP with your team.

CHAPTER 7: TRANSFORMATION

This chapter details the criteria for selecting a TP that will have a substantial, positive impact for you and your client. We will explore how to find ideas for account transformation and how to present your project, keep it on track and deliver results.

Assessing your client relationship

Before you start to work on the account transformation, think about the strength of the relationship you have with the client. Consider the level of trust you have, the way your team develop new opportunities and offer other products or services to the client. Mark on the client relationship graph, where you think you are.

Then separately ask your client to mark where they would grade you (download additional copies at www.rjen.co.uk/downloads). Then bring out your version and show where you marked the relationship.

If you are both aligned, that's great you have a good starting point. If it's not aligned, it's an important discussion point to talk about what the differences are and why.

Ask why they scored you where they did, what needs to change to improve the score, what do you need to do more or less of? Was there anything you could improve on or have done differently?

How you are scored gives you a valuable insight into how your business relationship is perceived. From there you can openly discuss how you will move up the graph; remember your TP could be the conduit for that. If lack of trust is due to a significant past issue, encourage your client to think of the future. For any TP to be successful, their level of trust in you will be very important.

A TP has to be bold, ambitious and aspirational. It should give you a twinge or two of concern about being able to complete it.

Your vision of success for your TP and the impact that the transformation will have on you, the business and the client must to be very clear. This vision will serve as a reminder for why you started the project in the first place. Your vision will help to keep you motivated and on track to achieve it if problems and challenges arise. If your vision doesn't excite you, then you've not selected the right project.

If that is the case, review it again, involve the team, explain why it doesn't hit the mark. Restart the brain storming process. TPs take time to complete and there will be bumps in the road to deal with along the way. Therefore, the prize has to be big, worthwhile and exciting!

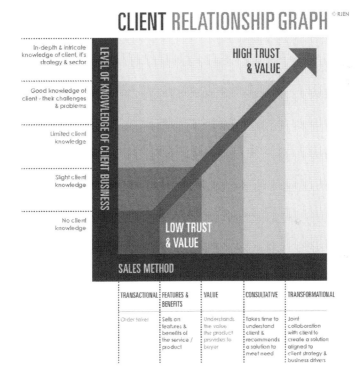

Let's define the dynamics of what makes a project transformational.

1. It offers substantial value to the client. It's aligned with their corporate goals and/or key business drivers.
2. It has to benefit your business too. Otherwise, it becomes unviable to invest time, energy and resource in it.
3. It has to be in alignment with the values of your client and your company.
4. It delivers progress in an area that your client is keen to develop.
5. It has clearly defined goals, results and outcomes which are bold and ambitious.
6. Both companies make it a priority and commit to it through investment; this could be people resources, premises, cash.

Using the research strategies from part one of this book, you will have knowledge of the future trends impacting your client's sector.

Combine this with your own knowledge of the client and list out three or four areas that you think would be of interest to them to develop.

If you're struggling, take a broader look into business trends over the next few years and see if any of these are relevant.

A quick internet search on business trends has thrown up the following:

- Augmented reality
- Artificial intelligence
- Values over bottom line
- Blockchain technology
- Big data contextualisation
- Ethics in algorithms
- Personalised marketing
- Employee happiness and wellbeing
- Increased remote working
- Smart cities

(Source: Adam Uzialko).

Are any of these relevant to your client?

Another option is to have a conversation with other executives in your client's business to gain different perspectives. Ask them how they see the future for their business, what trends and challenges will impact them.

Take time to understand their strategic plans. Ask, if you could wave a magic wand what would they want to achieve in their business over the next three years or longer term.

Review what you have done for other clients; have you achieved transformation elsewhere in the business which might not immediately seem relevant to your client? As you analyse your activities further, it might spark ideas where it could be relevant to them.

Attending conferences relevant to your client's sector and listening to keynote speakers about how they see the future might generate ideas. It could also help you to see your client's world from a more strategic perspective.

Sometimes the best ideas for a TP comes from outside your immediate team. Perhaps that's because they are less constrained by the art of the possible when they aren't close to the operational detail. Invite colleagues who don't work on the account and brainstorm ideas with them too.

When you have some exciting ideas, prepare a discussion document or presentation that outlines your project to share with your client and ask your leader for their input too.

Unable to find a transformational project?

An account manager was under pressure to find a TP in her client account. A few weeks past the deadline of having an outline ready for discussion, she still didn't have any ideas.

If you are stuck like this, and **only** after following through on all the ideas listed earlier, talk to your client about the concept of a TP. Explore if they are willing to work with you to come up with ideas.

The downside of this, is that if it's met with apathy it's killed before it even got started. If you have a meeting like that, always leave with the door ajar, with an agreement to go back and discuss it again if a better idea arises.

In the case of this account manager, she sold in the concept of developing a TP *without* any specific idea of what it might be. She purchased tickets for them both to go to a digital technology conference with the sole purpose of exploring new developments together, which could lead to a TP.

What to do if none of your accounts has a transformational opportunity?

I've yet to meet a chief executive or executive team member who doesn't have any challenges, or who isn't keen to think creatively about product development for the future. This is especially true if you are sharing deep and relevant sector insights and trends and bringing new knowledge.

Be bold, pick up the phone speak to the PA of the Chief Executive of your client and ask for 15-minute slots with each senior executive to gain their insights.

An experienced account manager that I was working with had key accounts with two retailers and had selected them both for TP opportunities. Over the course of developing their TP, it was announced that both companies were in separate negotiations to sell/merge with other companies.

Immediately the TPs were put on hold and her multimillion-pound opportunity plummeted to zero. Neither companies would invest time and resource into a TP with a merger in the air. This left her to review her other accounts, but she was sure that there was no opportunity in any of them.

This is when it's good to get a colleague to review the process of client evaluation and cast a fresh pair of eyes over it. This is what she did and in having a colleague challenge her assumptions it became clear that her knowledge in the sector of one of her other clients wasn't detailed enough.

The next step was to go back to the sector and company insights work (part one), to gain that detail. Insights are the foundational work to discover transformational opportunities.

Considerations to finding a transformational project

1. What are the rising trajectory trends in the sector that could offer opportunity?
2. What are the strategic goals and business drivers of your client where you could deliver improvements?
3. Speak with senior executives across different functions in your client's business for their perspective on challenges and trends on the horizon.
4. Consider emerging technologies that could impact your client's business to reduce costs or improve efficiencies.
5. Look outside the client's sector and market to see if there are developments that could be relevant to your client. You might

have other accounts that are creating innovation that could be adopted for your client.

Presenting your transformational project to gain traction

Once you have the outline of a TP, book a strategic planning session with your client to present and discuss it.

A couple of hours might be needed, because you've got some important ideas to share with them and you need to allow time for their input. This is about being proactive; you've prepped and you're keen to share it.

Ensure the right stakeholders are at the meeting. Those who have the ability to fully discuss the project, progress it and are able to make decisions and orchestrate resources to support its development.

The layout below is designed to provide a structure to maximise the impact of your TP presentation. Although it has similarities to the presentation outline for the prospecting meeting in part one, it is different!

Presentation/discussion structure

An overview of what you want to present and why. This gives a taster of your TP.

Sector trends - the bigger picture

Present your insights. Build the case for your TP, outlining current and future sector trends and how these link to the client's business drivers. Talk through the impact that these trends could have on your client's business, both positively and negatively.

Strategic thinking

Outline the thinking process that you have been through. Demonstrate your knowledge of their business and how you think their strategic aims and business drivers diverge from or converge with sector market trends and the possible implications of this. Your aim is to add value and educate.

Transformational project vision

Outline your TP, a vision and potential outcomes. Excite your client with a bold proposition of real transformational value.

Remember that the TP must align to their business drivers (such as reduced cost, increase efficiency and/or improved client experience). You also want your client to be emotionally engaged with your vision.

Do this by talking about how it will impact them and their teams and make life better for them all. As you present encourage their feedback and input, aim for a sharing of ideas; your and theirs.

Challenges, risks & lost opportunity cost

Show that you've thought through the challenges, risks and opportunities. how you would manage the project, timescales, any resources required.

Talk through the impact and opportunity that would be lost for not implementing the TP.

Show you considered potential blockages to success. Demonstrate your skills and expertise to find solutions.

Next steps

Ask for their feedback and jointly discuss the project. You might be asked about resources, have an outline plan to address this. The main purpose though is that you want them to be excited about the outcome.

Financial benefits

Create an outline Return on Investment (ROI) calculation based on a high, medium and low outcome of the TP. Alternatively, outline increased sales targets, costs reductions, improved efficiency gains or other financial outcomes that the project will deliver.

TP costs

Find a way to share the costs of the TP project. Talk through any resources you would like the client to commit to, such as people and funding. It's important that they have some 'skin in the game' that increases their commitment. If you are making this a partnership TP, you could suggest sharing costs and upside on a 50/50 basis.

Turn influencing on its head

We are influenced daily by subtle and not so subtle advertising. Through social media, by our work colleagues, friends and family, our own experiences good and bad. TV, films, music and books.

On the day of your meeting it's down to you to use your best influencing skills. Your task is to get your client to see how impactful your TP will be to their business. Your ability to influence starts with trust. How much your client trusts you will impact how readily they agree to support and become involved in your TP.

That's one of the benefits of using the trust/transformation graph outlined at the beginning of this chapter. It's a method to gauge their perception of how much trust they have with your company.

If trust is low, guide the conversation to focus on how to improve it. Encourage your client to think forward and not about what has happened in the past which might have dented trust. If trust is high then super, move on to the next step.

We often talk about how we influence others, but I like to turn that on its head and get the person you aim to influence to do the influencing themselves. I find it to be much more successful!

Here's how:

Aim to engage your client in coming up with their own ideas to influence their decision and commit to the TP. The way to do this is to ask them to think of how others (companies or colleagues in the business) might deal with the sector trends or insights you are presenting.

As they respond to that, they are coming up with their own ideas; and that's the point. Their idea is much more likely to get buy-in and follow through than an idea you or your team come up with.

Your skill is in aligning your TP with their ideas. If there is no similarity, then you talk through what you had in mind. Consider the merit in their ideas. Work towards either your project, with examples of how it could work, a blend of both ideas, or their idea on its own.

Another way to use their influence is to present three variations of your TP and discuss the pros and cons of each to see which one they prefer.

Ask for their input on how it can be improved. That way you are advancing the discussion by debating the project and finding a way forward. As if the principle of creating a TP has already been accepted.

In a situation where you are presenting a TP idea, you might not be seen as a person with influence, yet! You can overcome this by talking about the ideas and concepts of an already established expert whose expertise is recognised and relevant. You will need to be knowledgeable about their work and be able to reference it.

Example - Boost your business with an influencer

Your TP idea might be to manage the call centre that your client operates in-house. Your company runs small call centres for other clients, but not to the size and scale of your TP. You've been to a conference on best practice in call centre management and you highly rated one of the speakers. You get in touch and talk about the challenges of running a larger service centre. The specialist is happy to come and talk to your client about optimising call centre efficiency and help you set up the operation once your client has agreed to develop it as a TP.

Listen out for any objections that your client comes up with in regard to your TP and remember that they are your gifts as we discussed in part one of this book. Use probing questions to get behind the objection and really understand the rationale for it.

How to increase psychological buy-in to your TP

Ask your executive leader to call the client the day after you have presented your TP. The purpose of the call is to see how keen and committed your client is to the project and to reinforce how excited you and your manager are about it too. This increases psychological buy-in; they've committed twice, to you and now through the call, to your leader: in effect a double commitment. If they have any reservations or second thoughts, your leader can deal with those on the call, smoothing the way for a successful kick-off. It also reinforces the commitment from your business to the client.

The power of story

There has been a rise in our knowledge of how to make emotional connections and its importance in building rapport with people and improving relationships. Stories are a good way to do this because they help us to remember messages; we can relate to them and they are familiar to us. Many of us have been raised with a bedtime story routine.

Your TP presentation to your client is also a story. The next example I've seen work very well on a number of occasions. It shows how, sharing your struggles and aspirations, helps your audience to connect with you. We love to hear about the 'dropout to superstar' story. Is it because so many of those favourite childhood stories, from Cinderella to modern-day box-office hits follow this format?

An example of using story to good effect

Rick, an account manager at a global software company, was working on a TP. His challenge was to engage with a senior director, Phil, at his client's company to gain strategic insights on a project that he was responsible for developing. The information would enable the account manager to develop a better TP. Rick didn't know Phil. Upon asking around the office and checking social media, neither did anyone else in the business. Fortunately, the direct approach worked. Rick emailed Phil, explained his role and his project and how much he would appreciate his input. Phil granted him a short meeting. In preparation for the meeting, Rick and I brainstormed ideas about how to make best use of the limited time he had been given for the meeting.

What Rick achieved at that meeting went far beyond what we had planned! He used his own story to appeal to the director's emotional desire to serve a bigger purpose, bigger than simply providing the insights that could benefit both of their businesses. He talked about his aspirations to become a director of the company, how he had dealt with challenges and setbacks.

He outlined how he wanted to use the TP as an opportunity to showcase his skills and make a difference that would benefit both companies. Rick asked Phil how his career had developed and what challenges he had faced and what advice he could offer. This may seem a risky strategy for a meeting with a senior executive that you don't know. Yet, many leaders have a strong desire to help others, fulfilling a need to give back and serve a bigger purpose. Often prepared to give up their own precious time to do so. The story resonated with Phil, who, as any leader has experienced, had overcome personal setbacks to achieve success and offered to mentor Rick to help him achieve his career aspirations through the TP.

Success Tip

Share your story, your challenges and aspirations – people can relate to it and it might encourage them to help you.

Do's and Don'ts in sharing your story

- Do show your passion. Let it shine through, it makes such a difference.
- Do use examples from situations in your life, to illustrate your point.
- Don't manipulate the situation to get a desired outcome. Be genuine, be you.
- Don't be 'scared' to share emotion, as it's what connects us with individuals.

It is more acceptable in business today to talk about struggle and failure and how you dealt with it. The rise of the entrepreneur has helped this. It helps others to relate to you and that builds rapport. There is a caveat to this: if it makes you overly emotional in telling your story, find a coach to help you with that or share another one that has less of an emotional impact on you.

There is a formula for creating your story, which I came across in Carmine Gallo's book, The Story Teller's Secret.

This formula works well for emotional buy-in and you could weave it into your TP presentation.

This is his 7-step story telling structure

1. Once there was (outline the struggle that your audience can relate to, which builds a bond with the audience)
2. Every day (the struggle continued)
3. Until one day (you set a vision of how things could be better, but there is a big gap between where you are now and that vision)
4. What you could do – (if you achieved it this could happen or that could happen)
5. And because of that – (we did this)
6. And the outcome was – (the triumphant ending, how we overcame the struggle)
7. Moral of the story is – (end with what you learnt from it)

Example of how to adapt elements of this structure to your transformational presentation to your client

1. **Struggle** - We know how important it is to your business to find a trading partner for Europe that has a product range that is complimentary to yours. We know it's important because there is a big trend towards your clients restructuring their supply chains to have one central point of contact to manage all medical supplies globally. You've discussed your challenges with us to find a suitable partner for over 12 months. We understand the impact this is having on your business through slower growth, impacting the profitability of your business.

2. **Vision** - We have been thinking about this challenge and working on an effective way to overcome it for the last four months, speaking to many of our contacts and researching potential options and partners. We've been considering the upside in resolving this problem and estimate it to be in the region of $10 million in sales revenue.

When we realised it would have such a significant impact, we increased our resolve to find a solution. We gathered our most experienced executives in the business to brainstorm ideas. Through this process that we had a breakthrough, an idea that we wanted to share with you today in this presentation.

3. **What you could do** – Our TC is different because we have taken an unconventional approach, yet in every situation we have tested this plan, it stacks up and it provides a revenue stream and benefits. Let's take you through it, we think you'll be excited by it.

4. **And because of that** – Lets agree next steps (action) to be taken.

5. **Outcome** - The outcome of this plan is that it increases your revenues by over 25 percent in the next 12 months.

6. **Moral** - What we have learnt from our insights is that with our strong partnership combined with our knowledge of the European market and our insights into your sector, we have a breakthrough to transform one of your most complex business challenges.

If you were on the receiving end of this, wouldn't you be excited to hear more, appreciating the effort that has gone into finding a resolution? Would you be prepared to give up more of your time to discover the solution?

Success Tip

Once you have one TP under your belt, you can use the story of it to share with other clients. This can inspire them to consider a TP with you. Show them how you created a transformation for that client. The idea you had, how you planned it. Then the action you and your client took, the outcomes and lessons learned.

Other benefits of building story into your presentations

Paul J Zak at Claremont University has, through research, discovered that our brains produce a neurochemical called oxytocin when we are trusted, or receive an act of kindness. This makes us more co-operative towards the giver. For example, you treat me well, I'll treat you well back. Oxytocin increases our empathy towards others and also our ability to experience the emotions of others and to be inspired to take action afterwards.

His team tested the production of oxytocin whilst listening to stories and discovered that stories can change the brain chemistry of the listener. Production of oxytocin is increased when the story is told in such a way that it attracts the brains attention, such as triumph over struggle.

Here's an example. Think of a film where you identified with one of the key characters. You could relate to their struggle; you were emotionally invested in their story and you felt sad or happy in line with their feelings in the movie. It's the same thing when you tell a story that your audience can relate to. Most businesspeople will have had their own work struggles, so most likely when you tell a story that includes your struggle, they will be able to relate to it. This produces oxytocin and they will be more inclined to be empathetic towards you and respond with action.

Be bold with your transformational project

One of the boldest transformation projects I've come across is with a senior account manager in the technology sector whose client was a global drinks-producer. Through his insights research into understanding market trends and the client's challenges, he began to understand what was needed.

The client wanted to be able to engage directly with the consumer and build a deeper relationship with them, rather than the relationship being predominantly owned by the retailers who promote and offer the product for sale.

His TP was to develop the use of the Internet of Things technology to engage the consumer directly with the brand. This could be done by the consumer scanning their smart phone over the bottle label, where the brand could reveal a story about the drink, such as its production, cocktail recipes, or its heritage. At the same time this provided useful data back to the drink producer.

The technology, although embryonic was able to be developed and it became his TP. The client put resources into the project and the status of the relationship between the two companies has rocketed.

Getting access to executive time isn't easy!

We are all busy, so when you make the call to ask for input from an executive, be well prepared. Think through your approach and see it from their perspective. Why should they give up some of their busy schedule to meet you? It will have to be a good reason and you will have to sell it well. You have to think about what is in it for them. Return to your insights and find the rationale.

In the case of the drinks-producer mentioned earlier, this is exactly what he did before he approached them. As a result, he had a very insightful and useful thirty-minute video conference call with the commercial director who offered to support the project in any way that he could! Getting that session was simply down to being brave, calling him and presenting the TC. It's one of my favourite examples of being bold and going for it.

Account multi-layering

Never let there be just one person in your company who owns the relationship with the strategic key account client. It sounds obvious, but it happens too frequently.

Key accounts are ones that should you lose them it will have a significant, detrimental impact on your business. That could be financial loss now as well as loss of future earnings, especially if the client is growing. It could be reputational loss, or loss of an important case study that you use to win other new accounts.

If you are an account manager never believe you are better off being the only person owning the relationship. It might feel as if you have all the power and that it makes you indispensable to the company, but not only is it unprofessional, it shouldn't be the reason why the company keeps you.

It actually puts you in a vulnerable position. If for example your key contact at the client leaves and the relationship with others is limited, the solidity of the client relationship can be fragile. This may jeopardise development opportunities.

Instead, share your knowledge of the client openly with other colleagues and encourage others to be involved. Your colleagues may have a different perspective and come up with new ideas or opportunities which can be developed to enhance the relationship even further.

Encourage your leader to play an active and strategic role in client relationship development to support your efforts. This could be meeting with senior colleagues of the client's team to gather deeper insights. Ask your executive leader to debrief you of these conversations. They may provide useful snippets or knowledge that you can use to effectively grow the account and develop your TP.

To summarise this chapter, we have we have covered:

- Powerful ways to build a highly successful relationships with your client.
- How to find a TP.
- A framework for presenting and launching your TP.
- The hallmarks of a TP.
- Techniques to progress the relationship beyond its current status.
- Why story helps engagement with your TP.

CHAPTER 8: LAUNCHING AND LEADING

In this chapter, we discuss how to launch your TP, for full engagement with your client's team. We go through a plan that will keep your project on course to deliver exceptional outcomes.

Once you have a commitment to the TP from your client, it needs a leader to inspire, manage and deliver it. If you are the account manager, then that leader is you! Congratulations, this is going to be fun, challenging and rewarding.

For this project to be a success, you need a joint project team between you and your client. As you will be bringing this new team together for implementation, a joint kick-off session is recommended. It establishes the TP and is a good way to get started with clear communication, vision and ambitious goals.

Keep in mind that this joint project team is going to keep your TP ball moving across the field and into the goal. This is the team that you are going to be spending a lot of time with. Your ability to build relationships with them is a crucial part of the project's success.

The TP project kick off with your client's team

You have the opportunity with the project team to set the scene and get started on the right footing. Here are some tips for a successful first session.

1. Set out the compelling vision that the client has already bought into. Talk through the value it will bring to the business as well as the impact of not doing it. Be enthusiastic and excited about it.
2. Provide detail that relates to those attending the workshop and explain the importance of their skills in making it a success. This could be IT, project, operational, customer service skills.

3. Outline their role in making the TP a success, such as their expertise, commitment or experience.
4. Use the story outline detailed in chapter seven to build an emotional connection.
5. Outline timescales, resources and methods, along with how the project will be managed. Will you use a collaborative approach, with focus groups and regular reporting?
6. How might team members benefit from being involved, such as recognition and new skills.
7. Ask for their input on how to make the project better.
8. Talk through the challenges you foresee and ask for input on how they could be overcome.
9. Get into the details; make sure every team member is clear about what they have to do next.
10. Agree on next steps with timeframes.

Relationship essentials

There will be essential key skills needed to ensure your TP is a success. Communication is a high priority.

Outstanding business development, sales professionals and account management teams build positive and strong relationships with their clients.

This increases the potential of them being involved in discussions about future developments and this is achieved through excellent communication skills. They know just the right time and way to present information; good and bad. They think about solutions and how to present them and they've developed active listening skills.

The same approach is needed for the planning, implementation and execution of the TP. Leading the project with the client is a vital part of your role. It has to be managed carefully, respectfully and with an openness and receptiveness to new ways of thinking for progressing the TP. The TP has the potential to enhance your client relationship further, open up new opportunities, increase your leadership status and develop your skillset.

As you develop the project you may face new situations. Welcome these, as they are an opportunity for personal and professional growth and development.

Earlier in the book, I mentioned that going for bold transformation had to give you some small element of concern about your ability to deliver it.

This is because real growth starts at the edge of our comfort zone.

Until you push yourself, you won't know what you are fully capable of. Today I still seek projects that make me feel uncomfortable because I know they will give me more experience and knowledge which can benefit my personal development and I can share learning and experience with others.

Addressing what's in it for me?

When you gather your TP team together, some of them may be coming to the meeting thinking, 'What's in it for me?' They may be unsure of what they might be expected to do when they are up to their neck in work already. Show empathy for these situations. Consider, ahead of the workshop session how you will respond to such feelings even if concerns are not stated verbally.

Empathy and rapport

Part of good communication is addressing the points that everyone is thinking, but no one is verbalising. Showing empathy is such an underrated but highly effective leadership skill.

To show empathy in this situation means relating to how the project team might be feeling. You can do this by giving some examples of how you've been in similar situations and the positive outcomes you gained and how you coped.

Don't do this in a way that makes you seem like a superhero; to be empathetic you have to talk from your heart and be true to you. Look for non-verbal communication signs such as a nod or smile that demonstrates that what you are saying is resonating with your audience. In this way, you build their trust in you and it shows that you care about how they feel; all traits of a good leader.

The importance of influence and trust has been a theme of this book. Aristotle, the ancient Greek philosopher, considered there to be three aspects to persuasion and influence. These being Pathos – appeal to emotion, Logos – appeal to logic and Ethos – the trustworthiness and credibility of the deliverer.

Appealing to individual emotions requires the recipient to see themselves in the situation you are presenting to them, triggering a positive emotional feeling.

Emotional appeal can work equally well to trigger positive emotions. Feelings of well-being and a sense of purpose. We know that when we're faced with a new idea or change, we want to know what's in it for us as individuals. We think of the emotional impact it will have on us.

However once we consider that, we can then think of others who might be affected by it or benefit from it. I do this a lot; it's part of human nature to share. I've watched a good movie, read an informative book or been to a good restaurant and I think of others who would enjoy it too and recommend it to them.

That sense of helping others, even those we don't know can be seen in other areas, such as leaving reviews. There are over 600 million user reviews on TripAdvisor; you don't benefit from giving reviews other than gaining digital badges. It's another bit of proof that helping others is part of our psyche.

Now bring that into the equation when influencing others with your TP. Give them a reason to feel good about helping you, the business and the client. Appeal to their sense of purpose. How will it help the business to grow, secure jobs or provide opportunities for promotion? These are all worthy reasons to mention.

Here's how you can use emotional appeal (Pathos) together with logic (Logos) when pitching a new idea, such as your TP, to your client's team. In this example, a company (the supplier) is pitching their TP to their client's developers who are going to be involved in the project. Spot Ethos – the credibility of the deliverer in there too.

Example of pitching a TP (to an overworked team!)

The reason for it: Logic, or Logos

(Making sure it passes the 'so what?' test)

As demonstrated in this example below

The reason for the TP is because research shows that generation x and y prefer to bring their own devices to use at work. We know that this is an opportunity to increase revenues for both companies through the development of software that doesn't compromise company data, compliance or legislation. This will allow employees will be able to use their own devices at work.

The growth potential is estimated to be in excess of £100m in sales for your company alone. As you may know, we are a provider of software security solutions and already work with your company.

We have presented an opportunity to your senior executive team to jointly work on a project to develop this technology to lead the way in this field and to grow revenues accordingly.

Emotional appeal: Pathos

(Does it pass the 'What's in it for me test? How will it make you feel? Pride? Accomplishment?)

We know that you are the best developers for this type of cutting-edge work and you'll be recognised as working on one of the biggest and most innovative projects in this company to date.

Your knowledge and experience will grow as a result, which will be recognised not just by Human Resources and your leader now, but in the future too. It will stand out as an exceptional achievement in your career.

This project is pivotal to the growth of the company and is being sponsored by the COO, who is taking an active lead in it. This gives you the opportunity to build relationships at a senior level and to showcase your skills and expertise. You will have achieved something to be proud of.

(Plenty of emotional appeal used here)

How it will help others?

Achieving the outcomes of this project will make a real impact and difference to your company, delivering growth, job creation and job security. You will have played an important and vital role in making this happen.

In addition to this, the technology that we develop will help others to increase their work satisfaction and make life less stressful. As they will use their own devices that they are more familiar and comfortable with, it will make them more productive too. You will have been instrumental in making that happen.

You can see how using these steps would build a compelling set of reasons to be involved in the TP.

Ethos – Credibility of the speaker.

Share your own experiences, such as other projects you've worked on, people you've worked, teams you've led and how you achieved success. Share insights into your leadership style and how you like to work. You want the team to believe in you and be excited about working with you.

The power of newness

Your TP will be offering something new. A new outcome, a new result and there is a lot of power in newness. People queue for new products. Cinemas launch new films every week.

Household cleaning products have a new formula; even toilet paper has a new softness or strength. We have new fashion styles twice a year and there is always a lot of hype around this. There is something in the human psyche that likes newness. Apply this to your TP, include what makes your TP new, leading, bleeding or cutting edge. Detail the new outcomes that it will generate and show your enthusiasm for how exciting it will be to be involved in something new like this.

Overcome fears

Our primary fears are loss, rejection, hardship, change, lack of certainty and disappointment. Address these in your TP client workshop. Talk about what happens if the project faces difficulties or challenges.

Help them to see that you will work through it together and find solutions. If I hadn't learned from my mistakes in winning and losing accounts, I wouldn't have been able to write this book and share my knowledge with you.

Share a story of when failure helped you to achieve something bigger and more positive than the failure itself.

In addressing their fears, you are giving your team a balanced view of what might be. Don't, however let the potential downsides hang in the air like a thick blanket of fog. Your role is to inspire and encourage with enthusiasm. Share the facts and detail of your research, your project plan, vision and outcomes. Show them an exciting future that together you can achieve.

Genuine and sincere

In all areas of communication, be genuine and sincere, as people can see through it when it's not heartfelt and real. It will be your quickest way to lose credibility. Share your values, what's important to you and how you like to work.

I know it's a well-versed saying that you can't please everyone, so don't be disappointed if not everyone likes what you present or your approach.

Encourage your team to embrace diversity and different viewpoints because that will make for a richer and more vibrant partnership.

Project Schedule

Plan your TP in detail. This will enable you to focus and move forward on a daily basis. Be disciplined, take daily steps towards the successful outcome of your project. This is important in showing your commitment to the team and client.

I am a big fan of 90-day plans, where you detail your weekly steps towards your project goals and overlay with key milestones. The creation of your 90-day plan works backwards; it reverse engineers from your vision to where you are now. From the vision, you divide the actions into quarters, then into months and then into weeks.

From your stated vision, list the key outcomes for success and the reasons why it's important. From there make a list of key milestones along the way in a linear timeframe.

The next step is to detail the weekly actions that need to be taken to achieve the key milestones; this requires a level of detail so that when you look at it, you know exactly what you have to do.

For example, stating an action such as creating a digital store, is just too broad. Detail the 50 or so steps that get you to that point. This approach provides focus and encourages action. The more detail you provide, the more clarity you have on the actions you need to take, creating momentum in your project.

Your own 90-day plan can sit alongside any project software. It becomes your own personal detailed reminder of actions. Each milestone that you pass is a success marker along the way, allow a little celebration when you achieve each one. Share the success with the team, such as thank you notes, an early finish, or lunch out.

You can download the 90-day plan template at www.rjen.co.uk/downloads and find one in the resources section at the back of the book.

TP success Do's and Don'ts

Do:

- Hold regular and frequent TP review meetings with your team.
- Make sure each team member fully understands their role and responsibilities in the project.
- Select the best team for the project.
- Address problems and challenges as they occur.
- Encourage openness so that problems are quickly aired
- Maintain and refer to the vision and outcomes, as well as why it is important, especially during challenges that delay progress.
- Monitor progress against key milestones each month
- Commit to personally actioning the steps outlined in your 90-day plan on a weekly basis- even on days when you don't feel like it!
- Use emotional appeal and logic when presenting the TP to your team.
- Involve your leader to develop the relationship at a strategic level with the client.
- Keep your client involved and up to date with the project on a regular basis.
- Share good and bad news with your client about the project; this is a partnership where you work together to overcome challenges that cross your path.
- Consider what might take the project off course and have a plan for it.

Don't:

- Ignore any fears that your team might have about the project; you might not have immediate answers, so commit to reflecting on it and getting back to them.
- Stop others being involved in your client relationship where they can add value to it.
- Think you've done enough communicating; it's ongoing, it never stops!
- Ignore the signals that could push the project off course, such as staff asking to leave the project, lack of progress or less client engagement.
- Accept low standards, address them and raise the bar.

You will learn much from implementing the TP. It has many benefits, from strengthening the relationship with your client, to increasing the perception of your business as a strategic partner. It can also have financial and client longevity benefits for your company.

The challenge is to include ongoing transformation into the way you do business with your client. It then becomes the only way to work together because it is so powerful and effective.

If you apply this process once, get exceptional results and then say, "That was a lot of work, thankfully it's over now!", you will be missing the point. While going back to how things were before is an option, it isn't an option if you want to keep clients for many more years to come. Building more TPs into the account gives you the ability to grow it beyond expectations.

What is important, is continually keeping the account fresh with new TCs that lead to joint TP's that progress the client's business drivers and strategic aims. Achieve this via ongoing deep research into their sector and understanding the strategic objectives of the company. Use that knowledge to create new TPs.

As mentioned earlier, we have an insatiable appetite for something new and now that you have the methodology to do that with your clients you can make it happen. As the saying goes, you can then 'rinse and repeat'!

To summarise - in this chapter, we've covered:

- Techniques for a successful TP kick-off project with your client's team.
- How to influence through logic, emotion and credibility
- A 90-day plan to keep your TP actions clear and detailed for progress.
- How to successfully communicate your TP for engagement with an overworked team.
- The psychology for gaining buy-in to your TP.

CHAPTER 9: SUCCESS MINDSET

What you can expect in this chapter are proven techniques that will have a transformational impact on you, your performance and results.

If you follow everything in this book and don't read this chapter, you will know how to win big in sales, What you will learn here takes it to the next level and can be applied for better results in sales and other aspects of your life too.

Staying focused

If you have responsibility for winning, growing and keeping transformational accounts, you most likely understand that it requires a concerted effort and focus over a period of time.

Creating regular blocks of time for focused attention on your TP is important. This time should be free of distractions; no emails, calls or admin tasks. Take the time to focus your mind to think specifically about how the TP is developing. What is working well, what isn't, what is restricting its development and how could faster and more effective progress be made?

These blocks of time will allow you to reflect on your leadership of the TP too. Despite its inevitable hurdles, remaining positive, confident and continuing to inspire your team is essential. Involving them and consistently communicating with your team can help you overcome many challenges. You don't have to have all the answers and it's fine to say that as long as you work out how you will find the answers needed.

It might take effort to focus in this way as we are so used to distractions and being busy doing. But like improving any skill regular practice will increase your ability to focus and it will become an invaluable way to improve your effectiveness and performance as a leader.

Having reached this last chapter, you have learnt that being bold and taking action is what it takes to target your next big account win and deliver your TP.

Reading about it is easy; applying it is harder. Being committed to successfully getting your project across the line is what distinguishes the mediocre sales professional from the sales genius. In this chapter, I aim to show you how to be that genius.

Accountability

Asking someone to hold you accountable for your progress and to be your supporter will make a significant difference to the success of your work. This person could be a work colleague in a different department, a business coach or friend. It must be someone who won't let you off the hook when you face a challenge. Select someone who understands your goals, appreciates why they are important to you and is supportive of them.

The very fact that you have started a TP sets you out as different; you are taking a risk, breaking boundaries and pushing forward. Having a supporter whom you can confide in, talk openly about any problems or issues that arise and get a different perspective from will be very useful.

You can use a version of the commitment pledge (detailed in chapter six), to think about how you want to work with your accountability partner.

Consider what will be important to you in the relationship, such as impartiality, confidentiality and constructive feedback. Your supporter should encourage you to raise your game too. It's like having a personal trainer; your performance will be greater when you are at the gym with them, rather than when you are there alone!

It takes a certain amount of bravery to step up and implement transformation, but there are no thanks for a half-progressed project. Like so many other projects you might undertake in different areas of your life, the last 10 percent can seem like the hardest part.

The excitement for the project will be high at the beginning and that will spur you on. It may ebb in the middle as challenges and barriers arise. Even when you are so close to finalising the project and you can see and almost touch the finish line, energy and enthusiasm can wane.

Your accountability supporter will make the difference. They'll encourage you, pick you up and help you cross the finish line if needed.

Your vision

Creating a mental vision of what you want to achieve has many advantages across all aspects of your life, health, career or finances.

In this instance, we are going to use the vision for the transformation. The vision has to have detail and clarity so that you can run it as a movie in your mind with you as the central character.

In the movie version of your vision, you might choose to focus on enjoying the accolades, results and positive feedback from your executive leader and your colleagues about the success of your TP. Imagine it happening in the present tense, at this very moment.

The most decorated Olympic Champion, Michael Phelps used visualisation. He contributes it to his success of winning 22 Olympic medals, 18 of which are gold. He created a mind video of his perfect race, including every detail; mentally repeating it daily and making the picture vibrant.

Run through this vision in your mind daily, make it vivid and as you do focus on the positive feelings that come from having achieved such a significant goal in your career.

It might make you feel excited and motivated, extremely happy, relaxed, on cloud nine, or even unstoppable. When you feel this good, the body releases chemicals such as serotonin, oxytocin and endorphins. As a result, your physical biochemistry changes.

The opposite of this, feeling negative, unhappy, anxious or stressed releases stress hormones, which over time can have a negative impact on your health.

The more you run through your vision of success in your mind, something amazing is happening in your brain too. You are creating new neural connections. The more you think about this vision, the stronger those connections become. These neural connections become hard-wired over a period of time and become a part of how you think and who you are.

The evidence

The Harvard Piano experiment illustrates this point extremely well. The experiment was conducted in 2007 by Neuroscientist Alvaro Pascual-Leone, who worked with two separate volunteer groups.

The first group went into the lab and learnt a simple five finger piano piece. They practiced it every day, two hours a day for five days, making the piece as fluent as possible.

At the end of each day, each volunteer in the first group took a transcranial magnetic stimulation test which mapped out the amount of the brain motor cortex development that took place. After a week of practice, the motor cortex of the brain relating to finger movement had increased.

The second group in the experiment played the simple piece in their head, imagining how their fingers would play the notes on the piano. That group also undertook the transcranial magnetic stimulation test; the results were surprisingly the same.

The region of the motor cortex that controls the fingers playing the piano expanded in both groups. The implication of this experiment demonstrates that mental training has the power to change the brain's structure. Stronger and faster connections are made, the more it is practiced either physically or mentally.

A subsequent second experiment followed. At the end of the experiment, the strength of the fingers of both groups was measured. You will be getting the gist of this now and you may not be surprised that both groups showed an increase in finger strength!

I use this technique in my everyday life. Not just in increasing the brain connections that link to my vision but in mentally rehearsing situations such as meetings. I consider how people might respond, how I'll tackle issues, the mood and tone of a meeting, the outcomes to be achieved

Before a recent sales prospecting meeting to explore delivering a program for a team of account managers, I mentally rehearsed the structure of the meeting. I included how I present; the engagement received, as well as the next steps agreed.

The mental rehearsal brings flow when the actual meeting occurs. I only rehearse positive outcomes and comments. I never focus on any negativity that might arise. Challenges yes, objections yes, because they are opportunities for clarity and growth. As you now know, I welcome those!

The other benefit that mental rehearsal of your vision brings is that it begins to change your beliefs about you. This happens through your reticular activator system (RAS), a part of your brain located above the spinal cord which connects it to the brain and its functions.

It is the gatekeeper between the conscious mind and sensory aspects of the body. It filters all the information that isn't necessary so that the important information gets through. The determination of what is important to you is based on your beliefs, wants and desires. Here's an example of how the reticular activator works.

Let's say you are thinking about changing your car. You've got a couple of options in mind and when you're out, you spot these cars everywhere. Your mind zooms in on them like a magnet.

Success Tip

Reinforce your vision by running the movie of it in your head. Connect that to the feelings of success, so it's both visual and kinaesthetic.

It's the same when your vision is clear, you've rehearsed it and it's important to you. Your reticular activator will filter information that is relevant to your vision and your beliefs about your success. What is exciting is that you can change your beliefs, rewire your brain, create new neural connections and alter your physiology.

When you run the movie of you being very successful, consider how you are behaving. Behave that way in your everyday life, this reinforces the vision of your success and becoming what you have visualised.

Mental rehearsal can be used in all aspects of your life; from rehearsing a great evening out with friends to moving into your dream home. The key is to rehearse it daily. The best times are in the morning as you awaken and also in the evening as you prepare for sleep.

The reason for this is that your brain waves are slower and you can more readily access your subconscious mind. This is important, because the subconscious mind is more powerful than the conscious mind. It can respond to strong thoughts about what you want to achieve that are part of your visualisation.

Managing your mind for success

Everything starts with a thought. You thought about the prospects you would target before you got in touch with them. You thought about what you will wear to work before you wear it.

We have thousands of thoughts a day, but have you ever stopped to think about your thoughts? Over the next 12 hours make a mental note of the quality of your thoughts. Are they positive and supportive of your vision, of you and your future? Are they mostly worries, doubts and frustrations?

Your thoughts change your body chemistry as previously mentioned and influence your behaviour. Your goal is to feel good; when we feel good, we perform better, we are motivated and life is easier.

If you find it hard to believe that thoughts change your body chemistry, think of a delicious food: a crisp apple or some freshly baked bread. Are they making your mouth water? Your body is increasing the production of saliva in preparation of the food you might eat, all based on a thought.

Think about how often you feel good. If you don't feel good most days, then managing your thoughts is a very good place to start. Read on for some very effective ways you can do that.

When a negative thought comes into your mind, acknowledge it and decide that you will deal with it later in the day. Until then, it doesn't deserve any more of your attention.

Alternatively: shine a light on it. Ask what is the worst that can happen, can you control that outcome? If not accept it and move on. If you can control it, decide what you are going to do about it.

If you are going to allow yourself to think negative thoughts, then allow yourself to balance those with positive thoughts.

Dwell on the positive thoughts for longer and most importantly let those positive thoughts change how you feel.

We can worry about things we cannot control, such as a future event that might not even materialise. In sales that can be worry over will your prospect say yes to your proposal. When you follow the methods in this book, you have done all you can but you cannot 'control' the final outcome.

Don't waste energy on such concerns. Instead, focus on what you can influence and manage. When you examine the worry, try to stand back from it, as an observer. Often you can then see how illogical it is and the worst that can happen isn't actually that bad.

I know there could be exceptions to this, but even in the very worst situations you can find reasons to be thankful and positive if you look for them. Worrying about something won't change anything, except making you feel worse in the process.

Perception is everything

Your experiences of the past don't have to influence your success now or in the future. Take massive action towards the goals in your 90-day plan. Taking action and moving forward is progress that feels good.

In part one of the book, we talked about the congruency of your brand and that of the company. Now there has to be congruency between your thoughts, your feelings, what you say and your vision. Unless of course, your vision is of a grumpy, negative and miserable person!

Make your thoughts happy, uplifting and inspirational as your lead your team to success with your TP. We become what we think and right now, we are the outcome of our thoughts.

Think of your mind as a computer hard drive, negative thinking is akin to a virus. You have to clear that before the computer will work effectively and you as a person thrive.

Remove worries and self-doubts that sabotage your success and put effort into managing your mind. Repeated daily practice over 30 days will see change. Keep it going for 90 days and you will reach a point when you have a complete paradigm shift.

You'll become surprised by a negative thought as it won't be your norm anymore. You will wonder where it came from as they are now a rare occurrence.

Your vision and goals and why they are important will help you to remain focused, but only if you are disciplined in referring to them regularly. Give yourself time to reflect and review them. Keep the images of them strong and vibrant, as Michael Phelps did.

Managing your mind can be challenging to master. Master this along with the delivery of sales transformation and you will be an inspiring and successful sales leader and genius.

Making tomorrow better

If you are not happy with how your life is today, commit to changing it.

Use the techniques outlined in this chapter, create a vision and mentally rehearse it. Make sure you have congruency between thoughts, words, actions and behaviours.

Commit to it daily and it won't be long before your world is a positively transformed place.

To summarise this chapter, we have covered:

- Techniques to overcome personal and emotional blocks to transformational success in all aspects of life
- The importance of having a vision and how to use mental rehearsal for success
- Demonstrated that you can rewire your brain through thought alone.

FINAL SUMMARY

You have been through each step of my sales methodology. Vision, insights, transformation, application and leadership (The VITAL process).

Vision – Create a vision of success for that significant account win or for transforming an account you manage

Insights – Gain both company and sector insights that provide a detailed perspective of the trends, challenges, business drivers and strategic aims of your prospects and/or client accounts

Transformational concepts and projects – Using insights and value exchange meetings to create a TC and project

Application – Collaborative execution of the transformation

Leadership – Leading the joint TP team with essential skills

These combined steps will create a huge positive change in the relationships with your clients and the growth of your key accounts. This will enable you to win big valuable accounts, even if your company is smaller than your competitor and even in the uncertain times we face.

You will deliver impressive and meaningful results. You also have ways to overcome any obstacles or doubts that your mind puts in your way. So, what are the next steps?

Next steps

In this book I have shared my experience and knowledge in winning big sales. You my reader, can win big too. I would encourage you to:

- Read, annotate and re-read this book
- Litter the book with bent pages and post-its full of insights
- Take action with a transformation that makes a positive difference to your client, your company, your team and you.

If you're excited about delivering amazing transformational results and need some support you can;

- Book a transformational sales strategy session or workshop for your business.
- Book a VITAL talk for your sales or account management team.
- Book a keynote session at your sales conference

You can contact Rebecca through her website www.rjen.co.uk or via social media

https://twitter.com/rjenresults

https://www.linkedin.com/in/rebeccajenkins01/

https://www.instagram.com/rebeccajenkins.rjen/

ACKNOWLEDGEMENTS

Thank you to my family, my biggest and most important win. Your support and encouragement to go after my big vision inspires me.

This book is dedicated to my husband and children, Marcus, Amara and Callum as they step into and develop their own business ventures.

Thank you to my clients, colleagues and suppliers. Many of you have become special friends as we traverse the challenges and opportunities of business together.

ABOUT REBECCA

In growing and leading a £55 million sales turnover business, Rebecca understands the pressures of achieving high performance growth in an extremely competitive market. She shares her experience of winning and retaining big valuable accounts for many years.

Later selling the business to an international PLC Rebecca became their UK sales director before setting up her next business.

A consultant, speaker, coach and trainer, Rebecca works with businesses large and small, to develop their sales and marketing strategy and expand their competitive advantage. Using her five step VITAL methodology, she also works with ambitious sales and account management teams to achieve transformational sales results.

Visit www.rjen.co.uk/rebeccajenkins

RESOURCES

Template 1 – The Sector Analysis Template of your existing clients

Company	Size of Company	Financial Viability	Sector
Client name	Turnover	Gross margin or profit margin % on that client	What market sector is your client in?

Scoring Key out of 10 for Templates 2a and 2b

0-3 = low/no answers   Shade box red

4-6 = medium/possibly/potentially answers   Shade box amber

7-10 = high/yes answers   Shade box green

Template 2a - Sector Attractiveness
(You are scoring your answers out of 10 and red/amber/green)

MARKET ATTRACTIVENESS	
Sector: (note your target sector here)	Score (1-10) equating to Red/Amber/Green
Market Share What is our share of the market in this sector and is there room for growth and scalability? Answer low, medium or high.	
Growth To what extent is this sector growing? Is the market mature, growing or in decline?	
Risks Are the risks of operating in this sector low, medium or high?	
Financial We have the resources to invest in this sector and achieve acceptable return on investment	
Prices Are prices and margins under pressure in this sector?	
Summary (Add the score in each box, divide by 5 and shade the box according to the scoring key)	Total = Divided by 5 =

Template 2b - Capability to Convert
(You are scoring your answers out of 10 and red/amber/green)

CAPABILITY TO CONVERT	
Sector: (note your target sector here)	Score (1-10) Red/Amber/Green
Competitive Advantage Do we have a strong competitive advantage?	
Sector Expertise Is our knowledge of the sector detailed, do we know its challenges and are we regarded as a lead supplier in this sector?	
Innovation/Added Value We can evidence innovation or added value through case studies, testimonials or reports	
Performance We can evidence that we deliver performance benefits through case studies, reports, testimonials	
Position of brand leadership We are regarded as a lead supplier to this sector	
Summary (insert most dominant colour)	

Template 3 – Company and Sector Insights

Company Name	
Contact name and job title	
Website	
Address	
Parent company	
Financial Status, current and last 3 years Turnover, profitability, credit rating, public/private Who are the directors? (make a note of their name to connect/follow on social media)	
Is the company of a size and scale that is viable from a business opportunity perspective? (Does it fit with the sweet spot from your first analysis of your existing clients and financial analysis?)	
Vision, mission, strategy Review company accounts/website/articles/press releases for information that gives you a good understanding of their goals, culture and values/new product developments/clients/service offering/challenges/problems that they are talking about/awards won/senior appointments	
Contact name and details, job title, LinkedIn profile of decision makers/directors	
Are they talking about any specific challenges or trends that you didn't capture in the sector analysis	
Who is the current provider of the services/product you provide and what do they offer that you don't?	
Length and value of their existing contract (if applicable)	
Their position in market, top tier, mid-tier, emerging,	
What are their key business and economic drivers, i.e. efficiency, growth, disrupting a market, market share, occupancy levels, machine downtime?	

Sector Insights *Note: Reading trade/professional journals & reports relevant to the sector will provide this information, as well as attending relevant seminars, workshop and conferences.*	
What are the current sector trends?	
What challenges is the sector facing?	
What future opportunities are being discussed at events or professional associations about the future of the sector?	
Is the sector being disrupted by newcomers or new technology and how are companies reacting to that?	
If companies could have three wishes fulfilled to resolve challenges and improve the sector what would they ask for?	

Template 4 – Personalised Letter

Letter content example	Benefit of including it
Dear	
The cost of recruitment in Poland is increasing	*Letter heading to get attention*
I recently read in your company accounts that you are expanding your operations into Poland.	*Shows you've done your research and personalised the letter to the company and that it is relevant*
I wanted to share with you our research on why the cost of recruitment in Poland is higher than in other European countries. Our research also provides effective methods for mitigating those costs and still achieve a 99% job fill success rate.	*Reasons why they should meet you. You are offering insights into a challenge they are going to face. Positioning you as experts in this area. You show that you have a potential solution to the problem.*
We have been successfully recruiting in Poland on behalf of British companies for the last 5 years.	*Gives you credibility*
Brian Smith Operations Director of Ace Chemicals said 'their specialist knowledge of Poland has enabled us to have a very successful recruitment record there'.	*A testimonial builds trust*
I look forward to taking you through the report and explaining the top 5 ways to overcome these challenges. A short meeting either in person or video conference is all that is needed.	*You are offering value, there is no hard sell.*
I will call you next week to arrange a meeting.	*Clear next steps*

Template 5 – Selection criteria for priority accounts

Client Questions	Response Red = no Amber = maybe Green = yes
We know their strategic goals and business drivers	
We know the trends in their sector and their potential impact	
The account has grown year on year since we first had it	
The account has profitable growth potential	
There are elements of their work that we aren't doing but we could	
They have potential future challenges or opportunities we could help them with	
We can add more value to their business	
They are financially sound; we have analysed their financial position and it meets our criteria	
They have a positive view of us	
The relationship is strong and they are pleased with the work we do for them	
They are receptive and open to new ideas and ways of working	
We make a sound/acceptable return on the account	

	TP vision	Week 1	Week 2	Week 3	Week 4	Week 5	Week 6	Week 7	Week 8	Week 9	Week 10	Week 11	Week 12	Week 13
TP vision	To put the first commercial natural gas truck on the road & to have it operational within 24 months which demonstrates our ability to add value and be innovative to our client													
Milestones		Q1 Milestones				Q2 Milestones					Q4 Milestones			
		Prepared Manufacturer Brief	Brief Issued	Truck manufacturer research completed	Proposals received	Proposals evaluated	Shortlist manufacturers selected		Final manufacturer selected	Terms and conditions agreed	Schedule of work for discussion and decision	Schedule of work agreed		
Weekly Actions		Meet with fleet engineer to discuss potential truck manufacturers to contact												
		Brainstorm with fleet engineer the scope, requirements and vision to create a briefing document												
		Ask admin support to collate contact details												
		Speak to truck manufacturers to sound out their initial interest in project.												

Printed in Poland
by Amazon Fulfillment
Poland Sp. z o.o., Wrocław

64225339R00078